The Art of the Blade

History & Practice

retzev

THE ART OF THE BLADE
Copyright © 2022 by Retzev
—First Edition—
ISBN-10: 0-9980654-4-7
ISBN-13: 978-0998065441

All rights reserved. No part of this book may be reproduced in any form without prior, written permission from the publisher or author, except in the case of brief quotations in articles or reviews.

The material in this book is intended for educational purposes only. No one should undertake the practice of self-defense or healing without qualified instruction and supervision, and an awareness of the criminal and civil limitations on the use of force in self-defense and the practice of medicine. Physical combat is an inherently dangerous activity. Medical diagnosis and treatment should be provided by qualified healthcare professionals. The author, publisher, and distributors are not responsible in any manner for any injury or liability that may result from practicing—or attempting to practice—the techniques described herein. Any application of the information contained in this work is at the reader's sole and exclusive risk. Because of the danger of injury to oneself and others, prior to engaging in any type of self-defense program it is advisable to consult both a professional martial arts instructor and a licensed physician.

This book was printed in the United States of America by Stirling Bridge Publications; a publisher specializing in works dedicated to exploring the power of one.

stirlingbridgepublications@usa.com

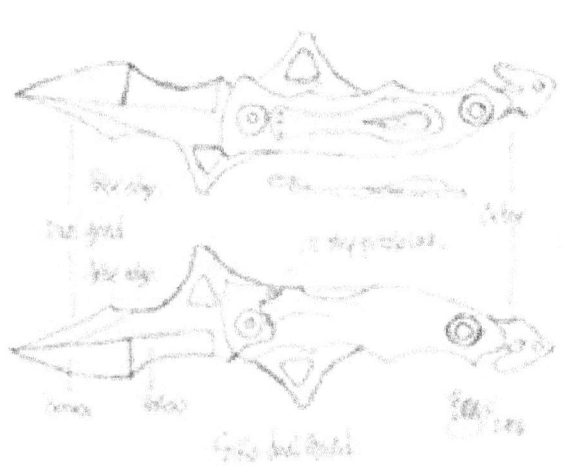

Dedicated to:

Bram Frank

Master blademaker,
Master knife-fighter,
Master instructor,
and true gentleman.

TABLE OF CONTENTS

	Foreword (Mish Handwerker)	1
I	Introduction (Thomas Lehmann)	5
II	Origins of the Tool (Amy Kirschner)	20
III	Origins of the Art (John Ralston)	28
IV	The American Tradition (Vince Oller)	35
V	Remy Presas (Tony Torre)	47
VI	Bram Frank (Dan Anderson)	59
VII	Choose Your Tool (Dave Giddings)	68
VIII	Choose Your System (John Ralston)	78
IX	Body Shifting (Eric Filippenko)	93
X	Give & Take: The Cornerstone (John Ralston)	104
XI	Patterns of Force (Chad Bailey)	115
XII	Switch and Decision Points (John Ralston)	125
XIII	The Rest of the Story (Amy Kirschner)	132
XIV	Unarmed Defense (Edessa Ramos)	143
XV	Knife to a Gun Fight (John Ralston)	153
XVI	Armor and Shields (Bruce & Chris Chiu)	161
XVII	The Sword (Jason May)	168
XVIII	Aftermath/Less-than-lethal (Tom Gallo & Ed Frawley)	176
IXX	Commandments of Steel (John Ralston)	183
XX	Make it Your Own (Brian Zawilinski)	190
XXI	The Words of the Master (Stephen K. Dowd)	194
	Appendix A (Selected Designs)	217
	Appendix B (Selected Endorsements)	221

FOREWORD

♦Mish Handwerker♦

—Washington—

When I was approached to write the foreword to this book, I felt honored. Forewords are usually written by famous people, or those considered to be the best-of-the-best, and, since I don't consider myself to be either of those, let me tell you a bit about my journey and how I got involved in Modular.

I began my martial arts journey over thirty years ago, circa 1990. A majority of that time has been focused on Ryukyu Kempo and Kyusho-Jitsu (pressure points). About a year or so into my studies, an instructor suggested I begin learning a weapon. Having a practical mindset when it comes to self-defense, I chose the stick. This decision came mainly from my thinking at the time that if I didn't have a stick on me when I needed one, I could always find something similar to use.

Access to an Arnis instructor was limited at that time, but one of my fellow students had attended a few Modern Arnis seminars with Professor Remy Presas, so he brought me up to speed on the basic strikes, a handful of disarms, and both single and double Sinawali. This basic foundation allowed me to stumble through a few training sessions with Professor Presas at several "Big Three" seminars [Remy Presas, George Dillman, Wally Jay], but it wasn't until October of 2000 that I made the decision to really *own* my education in the stick.

Once back home, I found an instructor almost immediately. He eventually introduced me to Professor Dan Anderson, from whom I learned a great deal. However, it wasn't until 2005 that I got a call from Professor Anderson, who told me he was doing a seminar with this guy named "Bram Frank" and wanted me to record and edit it for a DVD.

According to Dan, Bram did a bladed version of Modern Arnis; therefore, their event would be an impact *and* bladed tool seminar. This was the precursor event that eventually sparked the "Stick and Steel" seminars which Dan and Bram did together for years.

Though I didn't actively participate in the seminar, I was intrigued by what I saw. Here was an individual who was showing with a blade what we were pretending to do with a stick. I was instantly hooked. From then on, between Gresham and Eugene, Oregon, I tried to attend every seminar Bram taught here in the Pacific Northwest. I eventually began making my way to Spokane, Washington, for his weekend seminars as well. I once drove *eleven* hours round trip with a student of mine just to attend a two-hour Friday night session because I couldn't get the weekend off to attend the entire camp.

I became an official Modular instructor in 2012. At that time, most of the instructor camps were held in Florida. Living on the opposite coast, I was able to talk Bram into holding an instructor camp the next time he visited Eugene, explaining to him I had the money to pay for *either* the camp *or* a trip to Florida, but not both. He agreed to do it as long as I was able to get a few others to attend. I made sure to get those people signed up.

The fundamentals of Modular have changed my martial arts forever. Primarily a Ryukyu Kempo/Kyusho-Jitsu practitioner, Arnis gave me flow, but Modular and Bram's knives gave me practicality with a tool. I was never taught how to properly step, turn, or body shift when learning kata. However, after incorporating the stepping and body-shifting taught in Modular, my kata became more stable, improving myself defense. And the fact that Bram's tools, bladed or not, are designed to also be used closed, spoke to me as a kyusho person, knowing I could still hit pressure points while utilizing an every-day-carry (EDC) tool.

In early 2021 Bram asked me to be the inheritor of Modular and everything associated within CSSD/SC. I know that with this honor comes a great responsibility; one which I am fully willing to own. As a martial artist, I have always identified as a Kempo and Kyusho person who studies the *blade*, but as time has gone by, I have begun to see myself as a Kyusho and *blade* guy who studies Kempo. Bram's legacy will continue with me, Amy Kirschner (as Senior Advisor), and our official chronicler, Peter Hobart [sometimes collectively referred to as: "the Modular Triad"].

This book is part of Bram's legacy and of the Modular system he developed. It is my hope that this work will provide you with insight into both the history of the blade and the powerful principles of Bram Frank's Modular system.

—Mish Handwerker

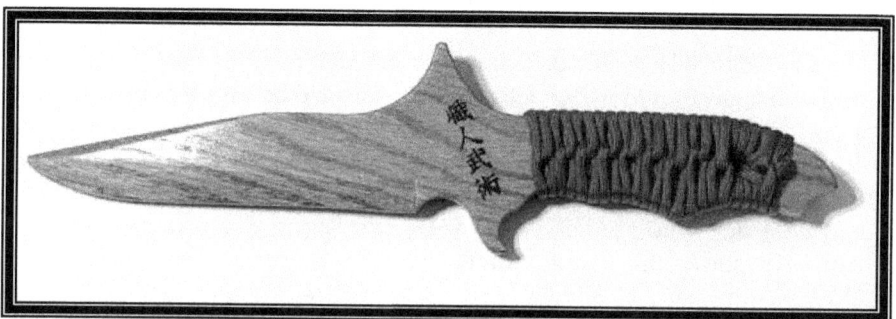

I. INTRODUCTION
Is This The Book For You?

Like most potentially life-or-death matters, when it comes to the art of the blade, it is better to know *one* thing well than to have a loose grip on a hundred. As a result, this work is unapologetically oriented toward a single approach: **Bram Frank's Modular Blade Concepts/Martial Blade Craft (MBC²)** program, often simply referred to as: **"Modular."**

The reasons for this preference are legion: From Bram's years of study at the hands of such legends as Modern Arnis Founder Remy Presas; to his decades of experience teaching his method to military and law enforcement personnel all over the world; to his expertise as a blade designer; to the fact that his system contains several components that are unique in the world of edged tools. But at the end of the day, this decision comes down to one critical factor: ***It works.***

MULTIMEDIA—MORNING COFFEE WITH BRAM

Most instructors agree that the martial arts are best taught in person, but during the global pandemic which placed the planet in a state of almost permanent lockdown during the writing of this book, everyone was forced to enter into the virtual world to some degree. In this regard, video of the Modular System at play can be an invaluable resource.

A good place to begin is with the vast library of clips available at: **bramfrank.pivotshare.com**. For example, the segment entitled, "*Abaniko Double Action*," explains the design that appears in the middle of the logo on the previous page. Over a hundred other topics may be found here as well, including the following free titles (which are linked to appropriate sections of this work using the Greek lettering system):

α. Modular Red Yellow Blue Black White
β. Ergonomics and Grip/Reverse Grip
γ. Perspective is Everything
δ. What's a Bramp?
ε. Blade Shapes and Design
ζ. No Two Hands in Same Field at Same Time
η. Training Knives
θ. The Puzzle Lock
ι. Cutting
κ. Bio-Mechanical Function PCAT
λ. Body Shifting
μ. Roof Block, Slant Block, and Umbrella
ν. Number Six and Number Seven Cuts/Arcing Thrusts
ξ. *Redondo* Rounding Cut
ο. Reverse *Sinawali*
π. Disarming
ϱ. The Presas *Bolo*
ς. The CRMIPT
τ. I Like Steel

In the crucible of real-world combat, soldiers, law enforcement officers, and civilians forced to call upon these techniques report that the Modular System has performed superbly well.

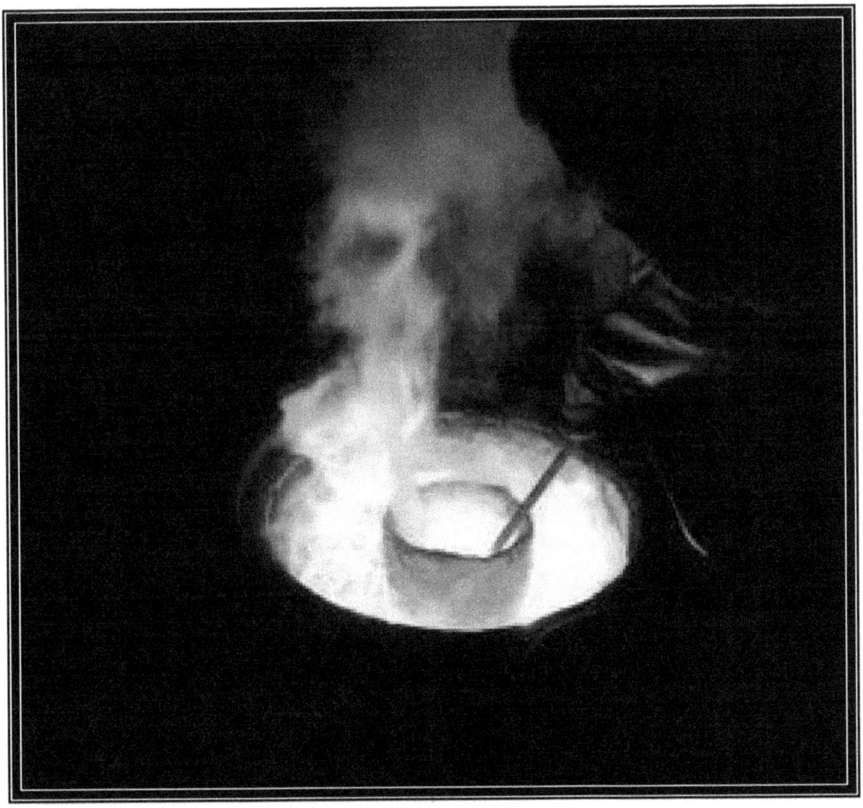

If you are looking for a more general survey of the world's many knife-fighting systems, then perhaps this is not the book for you (and the publisher will happily refund your purchase).

If, however, you are willing to consider the value of this particular method, then you are about to embark on a truly fascinating journey of heart, faith, and steel.

PRECEPT: BEWARE THE MAN OF ONE BOOK.

In time, as Bram is fond of saying, the information contained herein will develop into knowledge, and eventually, with sufficient study, that knowledge will mature into wisdom…

SYMBOLS
[α]

Modular is a martial <u>art</u>. The system's combat effectiveness—its *martial* component—is discussed at length elsewhere in this work, but for conceptual purposes, it is also vital to recognize its *artistry*. Bram—himself an accomplished visual artist—often expresses essential components of his system using imagery. And under the theory that a picture is worth a thousand words, the symbol on the back of this book was designed to try to capture some of that imagery in a single snapshot. Flip it over and take a look—your journey begins here and now.

As a threshold matter, the broad strokes of this image are based on the ancient *yin-yang/in-yo* symbol.

GRIP
[β]

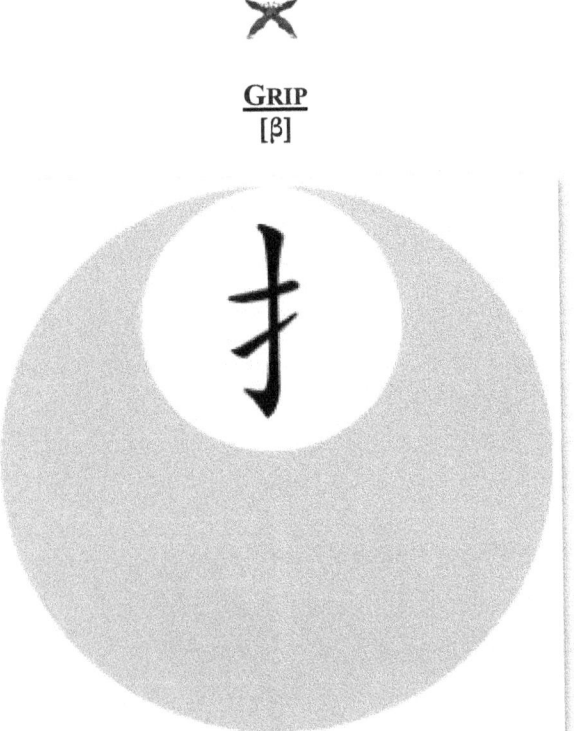

The character in the upper half (the yin "island" in a "sea" of yang) is the Japanese radical for "hand," and its passing resemblance to a knife with two hilts is the reason that it was chosen to represent the two possible hand grips for any bladed tool (forward and reverse).

According to Bram, in visual artistry, the color white allows for tinting, softening the overall appearance of the image, or adding focus to a single bright spot; valuable techniques for enhancing any work of art.

PERSPECTIVE
[γ]

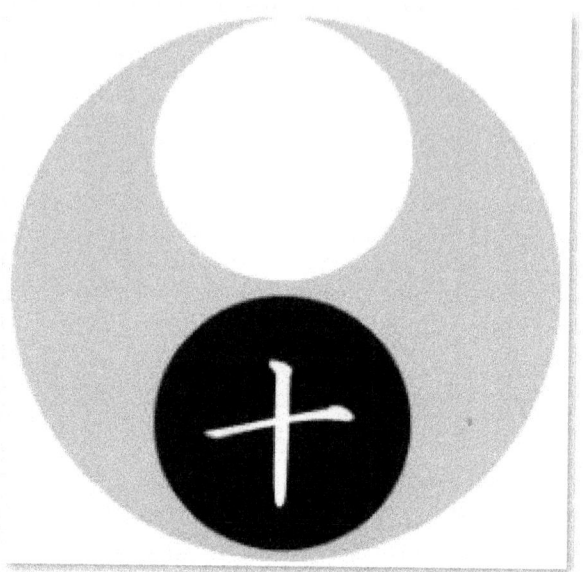

The character in the lower half (the yang "island" in a "sea" of yin) is the Japanese kanji for "ten," and it neatly quarters the four "perspectives" that Bram customarily teaches to beginners.[1]

According to Bram, in visual artistry, the color black represents shading—for adding depth and outlining, thereby making selected elements stand out—both of which are methods that truly help to bring a work of art to life.

---

[1] Together, the top and bottom characters may be read as: "Ten hands;" a fair assessment of the force multiplier that an edged tool provides in combat.

Perspective is a deceptively simple term—one which many students fail to grasp—and it lies at the true heart of the art, but one simple interpretation is to think of it as a way of facing the opponent and understanding the situation from the defender's point-of-view.

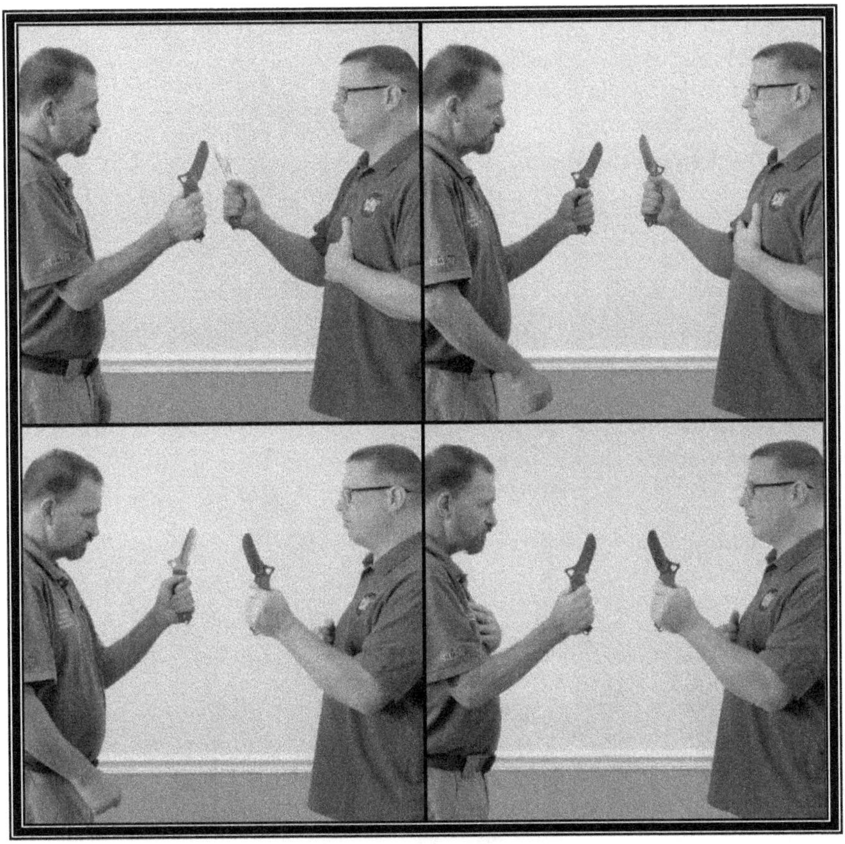

UPPER LEFT: STANDARD [RIGHT-TO-RIGHT]; UPPER RIGHT: BACKWARDS [LEFT-TO-RIGHT]; LOWER LEFT: MIRROR [LEFT-TO-LEFT]; LOWER RIGHT: BACKWARDS-BACKWARDS [R-TO-L].

† **Standard RH↔RH:** When the practitioner holds the blade in his right hand and the opponent also holds the blade in his right hand, this represents the most statistically common perspective, since right-handers account for about 90% of the global population.

† **Backwards LH↔RH:** When the practitioner holds the blade in his left hand and the opponent holds the blade in his right hand, this is *not* the mirror image of standard perspective—if it were, then the practitioner's left-handed techniques would always be following the opponent's moves—

rather, it is the perspective in which *the practitioner performs right-handed motions with his left hand* (which is a very important concept for naturally left-handed practitioners).

† **Mirror LH↔LH:** When the practitioner holds the blade in his left hand and the opponent also holds the blade in his left hand, this is mirror perspective. Perhaps the best way to make sense of this complex concept is to think of it as, *"the left-handed version of standard."*

† **Backward-Backward RH↔LH:** When the practitioner holds the blade in his right hand and the opponent holds the blade in his left hand, this is the perspective in which *the practitioner performs left-handed motions with his right hand.*

As a simple tool for understanding the four perspectives—at least in this incarnation—consider a highline open-to-closed attack. This attack can be directed at either the defender's left side (in the case of a right-handed attacker striking open-to-closed) or at the defender's right side (in the case of a left-handed attacker striking open-to-closed):

† In response to the right-handed attack on his left side, the defender can counter with either his right hand (standard) or his left hand (backward), depending on which perspective is in play.

† In response to the left-handed attack on his right side, the defender can counter with either his left hand (mirror) or his right hand (backward-backward), again depending on which perspective is in play.

AS THE FOX SAID TO THE LITTLE PRINCE, "HERE IS MY SECRET"

As Bram is fond of pointing out, Michelangelo's famous sculpture of the biblical warrior David was deliberately made to be viewed from below. As a result, when the vantage point is changed, the proportionality of such features as the head and arms, and the general appearance of the skeletal and muscular structure changes dramatically. It truly is all a matter of *perspective*, and for the discerning reader, herein lies the true secret of the art.

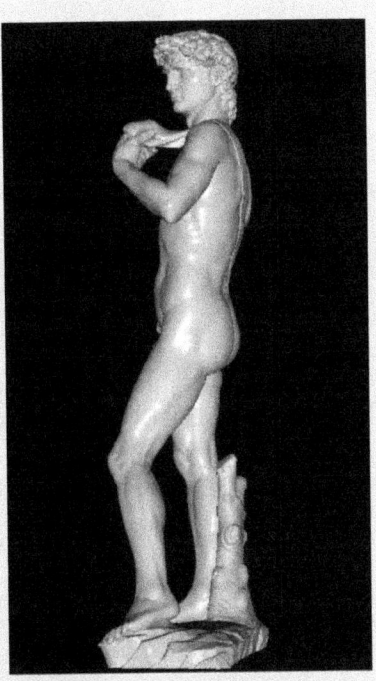

The Art of The Blade

TRAINING EXERCISES

RED: 1-4-12

† Red—a striking, conspicuous, primary color—represents the foundational "1-4-12" exercise, discussed in greater detail elsewhere in this work.

BLUE: 2-3-12

† Blue—red's cooler cousin in the primary palette—appears all around us in the background of nature (the sea, the sky) and represents the reciprocal "2-3-12" exercise, also discussed in elsewhere in this work.

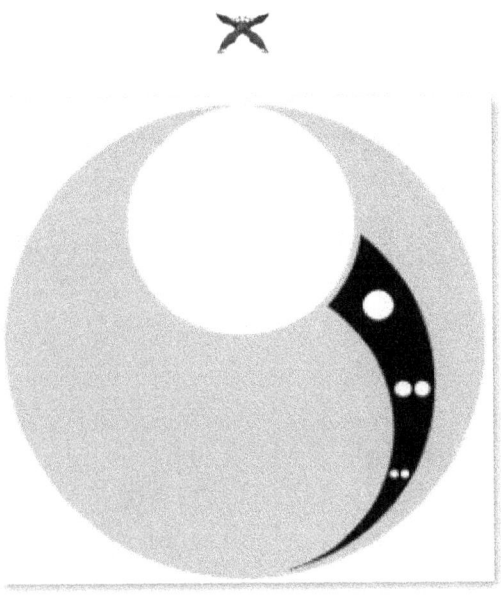

† Yellow—the mellowest member of the primary triumvirate—is sandwiched between red and blue, and represents the transitional "1-2-2" exercise, also discussed elsewhere in this work.

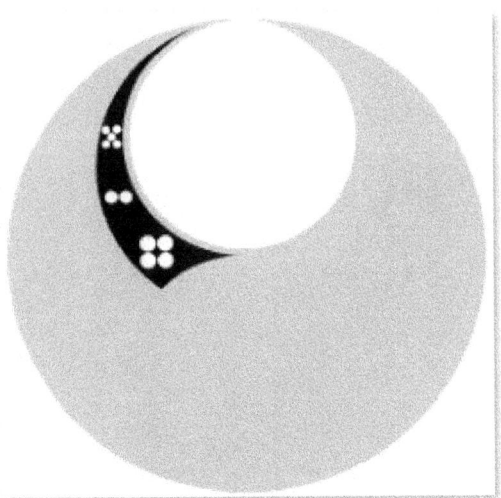

† Purple—a combination of red and blue—represents the "5-2-4" exercise, which shares elements with each of its 'parents' (1-4-12/5-2-4 and 2-3-12/5-2-4), but also adds the direct thrust into the mix (again, discussed elsewhere in this work.

The Art of The Blade

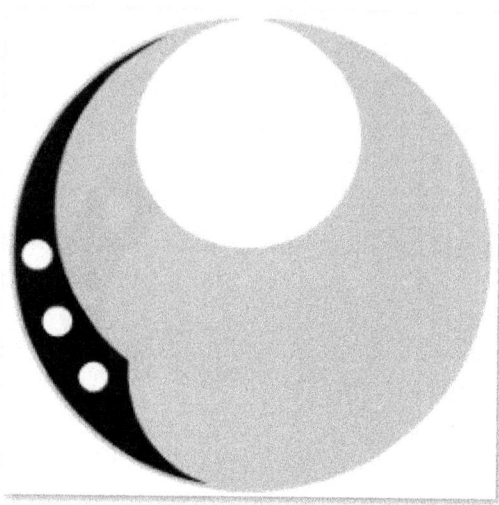

† Orange—the result of red (1-4-12) blending with yellow (1-2-2)—appropriately represents switch points (discussed in greater detail elsewhere in this work), and in this case, the three dots symbolize "S" in Morse Code.

† Green—the result of blue (2-3-12) blending with yellow (1-2-2)—appropriately represents decision points (discussed in greater detail elsewhere in this work), and in this case, the dash followed by two dots symbolize "D" in Morse Code.

♦ THOMAS LEHMANN ♦

— GERMANY —

I began my martial arts training at the age of fourteen, when I decided to study Taekwondo. Within a decade, I was a black belt and running three schools in Germany (two of them at American Air Force bases). During this time, I was a successful tournament fighter and won several national, European, and international championships. Many of my students also became successful tournament fighters and my main school was well known in Germany and abroad. Over time, I also studied several additional martial arts like Wing Chun, Hapkido, Aikido, and Jujitsu, but I was never able to find a street self-defense system which perfectly suited me. This all changed when I met Grandmaster Bram Frank for the first time during a seminar in Germany in 1992.

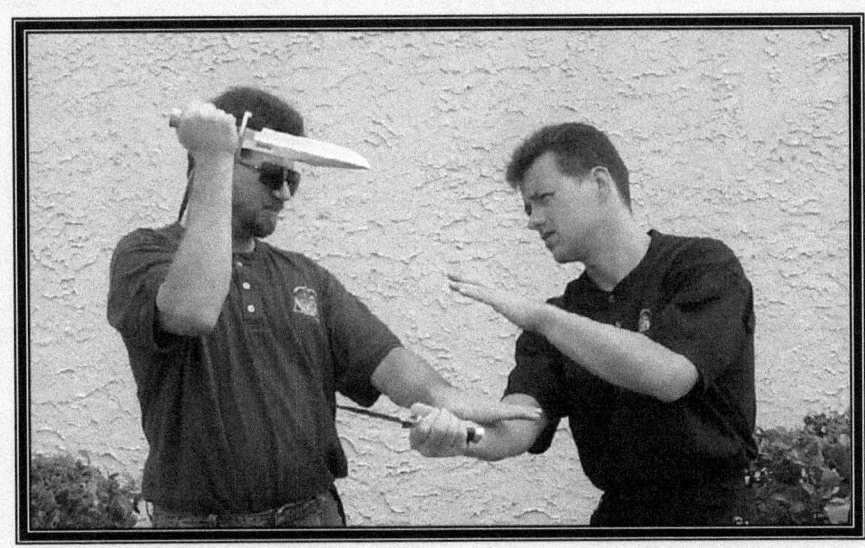

GM Frank introduced me to Filipino Martial Arts ("FMA") and his own system, **Common Sense Self Defense/Street Combat ("CSSD/SC")**. Since this time, I have studied under GM Frank, and also Professor Remy Presas, Guro Dan Inosanto, and various other Filipino Grandmasters. I found GM Frank's system to be so impressive and powerful that at the age of thirty-seven, I switched my focus exclusively to CSSD/SC. I then established CSSD/SC groups in Germany, Bosnia and Herzegovina, Indonesia, Afghanistan, and Thailand, and I currently travel all over the world with GM Frank to teach these and other organizations.

On one such trip in 2000, GM Frank and I were teaching in St. Petersburg, Russia. At this time, we were still using prototype *gunting* trainers—no round corners but sharp edges—and fortunately no blade. Throughout this trip, GM Frank used me as his *uke*, and after a couple of days, my arms looked like mincemeat! This earned the respect of the Russians—our training and exercises were very realistic... One evening we were presenting on a television program so we were dressed in suits with shirts and ties. When the producers asked us to give a demonstration, that was the end of my shirt! The sharp corners of the *gunting* cut right through my sleeves like water and even reached my skin! I still have some scars to show for it today...

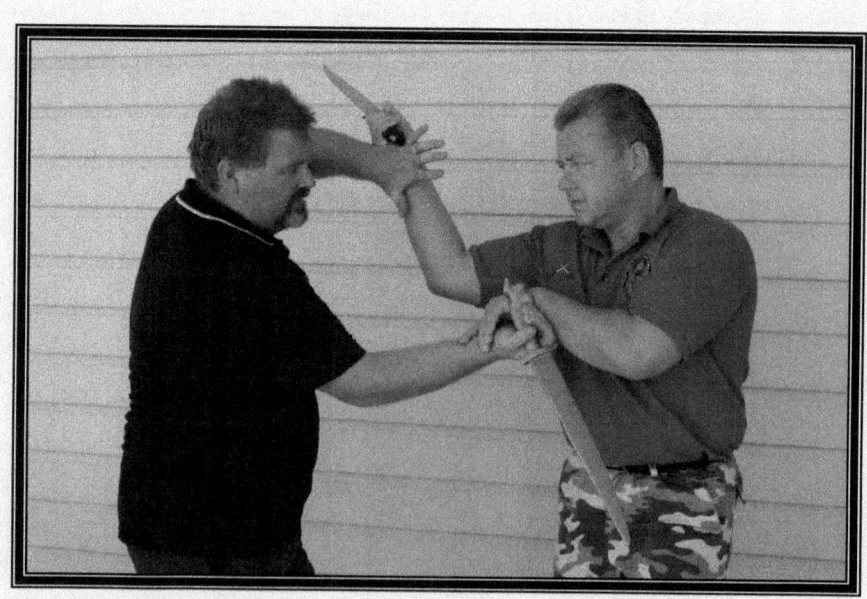

When Bram and I were at the seminar in Russia, we learned that St. Petersburg is a challenging place to stay! We had read that the tap water in this region was harmful and that we should avoid getting it in our faces. Bram was well prepared, as always, and had brought a water filter so that we could shower with tap water for the body and filtered water for the head and shoulders.

One morning I heard Bram yelling (I am one of the few people who has had the honor of sharing a room with Bram) and shortly afterwards he came out of the bathroom with the shower tap in his hand—it had fallen off on his feet during his shower! "No problem," we thought, "they'll give us another room." And they did, but in this room, the toilet flushed all over the floor! So we were moved to a third room. All seemed well until a few hours later, when we noticed that we could see each other's breath coming out of our mouths! It was February. In Russia. Eighteen degrees below zero. And the heating had stopped working…

One evening during this trip, we were invited to a private celebration in another hotel room. Our hosts served red wine first (which was delicious) and then switched to vodka, but before we could say anything, one of them said, "Let me clean your glasses to get rid of the wine taste for the vodka." He went into the bathroom, rinsed them with the toxic tap water, and then brought them back, saying, "Here you are—clean!"

We looked at each other, wondering what to do. If we asked for new glasses, it would be insulting, but if we drank from them, we risked the danger of contamination. Bram—always a wise gentleman—figured out the best solution: "We have enough medicine to kill any germs, let alone the strong Russian vodka itself, so let's be polite," he whispered. We accepted and had a great evening. We did not get sick. And we learned that the Russians are polite and friendly people who live in a tough environment. We still have true friends there to this day.

—Thomas Lehmann

II. ORIGINS OF THE TOOL
Matter Separators

 Imagine waking up in the middle of the wilderness, with nothing more to protect you than the clothes you stand up in. Many readers will be familiar with the 'rule of three'—three minutes without air; three hours without shelter (in adverse conditions); three days without water; three weeks without food—these are rules-of-thumb indicating how long one may expect to survive without a given necessity—but consider the *Outward Bound* instructor's version, which includes two additional bookends: Three seconds without blood and three months without hope.

> **THE RULE OF THREE**
>
> Three seconds without blood
> Three minutes without air
> Three hours without shelter
> Three days without water
> Three weeks without food
> Three months without hope

PRECEPT: REMEMBER THE RULE OF THREE.

Three seconds without blood? So if I cut my foot on a sharp rock, I'll bleed out in three seconds!? Of course not (but remember where you ran into that jagged piece of stone—you'll need it in a moment). Three seconds, however, is a good estimate of the interval between an initial hostile encounter with man or beast and the potential infliction of a lethal attack. Your very first order of business, then, is to arm yourself. And if no better option presents itself, it's time to go and retrieve that rock…

But what are the chances that my plane goes down in the wild or I get lost on a hike in the deep woods? Hopefully, slim, but keep two things in mind:

1. We are preparing here for the *worst* case scenario, and

2. This is the same circumstance in which our caveman ancestors found themselves, and it is in their hands that the object of our study—the knife—first began to take shape.

> **KING OF THE JUNGLE**
>
> Inspiration in many fields of study can be drawn from fiction as well as fact, especially when that fiction is based on fact. For example, many of the legendary and instructive exploits of that apocryphal sleuth, Sherlock Holmes, were based on the real-life studies of Dr. Joseph Bell. In a similar way, the adventures of the literary character John Clayton (better known as Tarzan) were based in part on author Edgar Rice Burroughs' experiences as a soldier, a cowboy, and a prospector in frontier-times, and it is no accident that the tool which gave Tarzan dominion over all the beasts of the jungle was his father's trusty knife.

According to Bram, a knife is, at its core, simply a matter separator. It is a tool designed to divide one thing from another. To sever strands. To carve wood. To slice fruit. To chip rock (incidentally, sometimes sparking fire). And in some cases, to cut flesh.

PRECEPT: A KNIFE IS A MATTER SEPARATOR.

Let us begin, as the King said to Alice, at the beginning: According to The Smithsonian, the earliest known 'matter separators,' were the so-called 'core-flakes' unearthed from the shores of Lake Turkana in Kenya in 2011, which date back 3.3 million years, to a time before modern humans. These tools were used by *Australopithecus afarensis* or *Kenyanthropus platyops* (Helen Thompson, *Smithsonian Magazine*, May 20, 2015).

From these early prototypes evolved the first flint knives used by Stone Age humans, and then on down through the metallurgical eras:

Bronze Age blades:

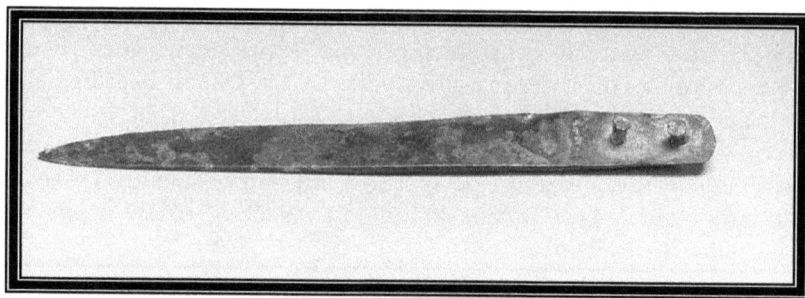

Iron Age cutting implements:

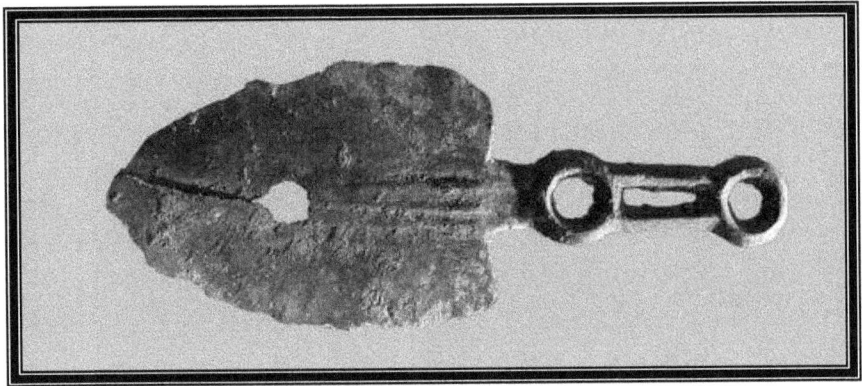

And eventually the refined steel from which modern blades are forged:

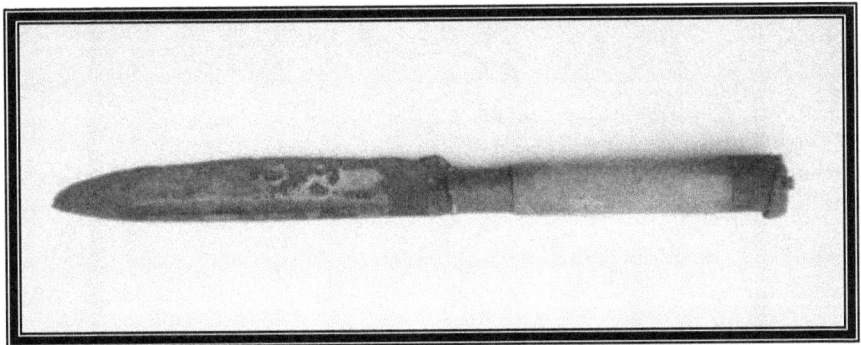

While it is not necessary for a knife-*fighter* to be able to *make* a blade, it is a skill still taught in various survival schools the world over, and a process worth understanding, if only through watching a few episodes of the amazing History Channel series: *Forged in Fire*. The simplified technological takeaway from this multi-layered field of study, however, is that the steel—or combinations of steels—used to produce the best blades should have a soft enough core to absorb shock without breaking and a hard enough profile to hold an edge.

But the choice of material from which to make a blade is only the first of many, including such variables as shape, length, curvature, weight, balance, grip, and finish, all of which depend in large part on the intended use of the tool. In the end, however, they all have one thing in common: They are tools designed to separate matter.

DAMASCUS STEEL

Damascus steel—originally forged in the Near East in the Seventeenth Century—is made from ingots of wootz and is characterized by distinctive patterns of banding and mottling reminiscent of flowing water. It can be forged into tough, shatter-resistant blades capable of being honed to a sharp, resilient edge. While some think that the secret to producing this exceptional material was lost in the mid-Eighteenth Century, Bram maintains that such modern smiths as Ed Schempp, Steve Schwarzer, Barry Gallagher, and John Davis have resurrected the art back to its highest standards and have taught many others to learn and use this art.

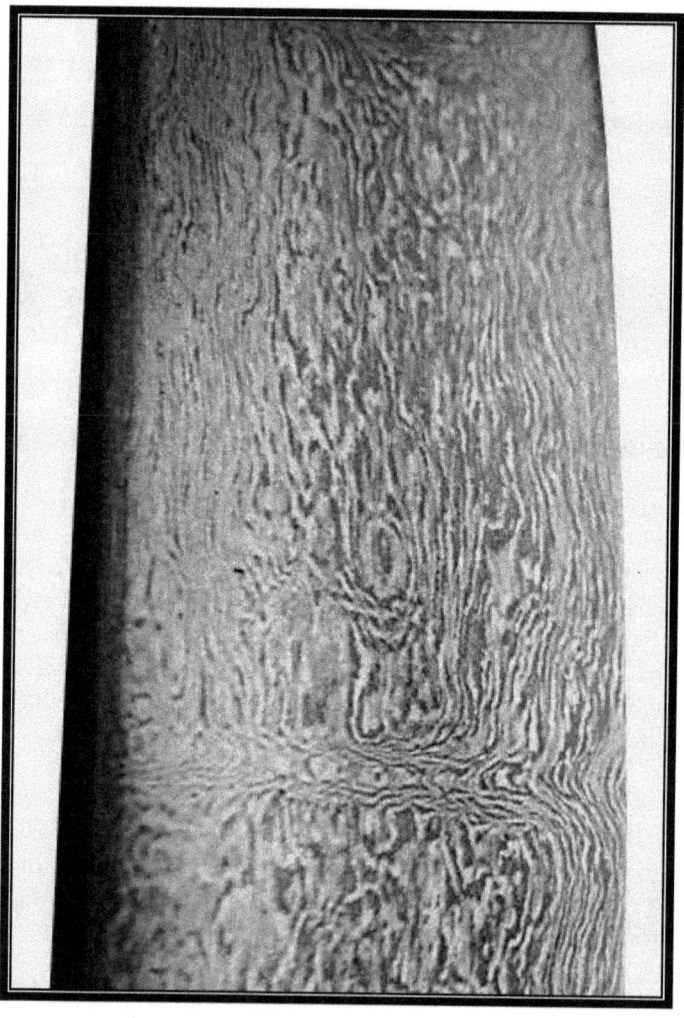

PERSPECTIVE—THROUGH THE LOOKING GLASS

A wise master once said to his students: "Let me be an example to you, if only of what *not* to do…" In many ways, we can learn as much by avoiding the mistakes of others as we can by emulating their successes.

No other section of this book has endured as many rewrites as this one, for two main reasons:

1. **It is vitally important:** In fact, during the editing process, Bram called late one night and asked out of the clear blue: *"What is the key to Modular?"* After offering up such conventional responses as, "To teach the safe and effective use of edged tools?" or "To ensure that the bladed aspect of Remy's art lives on?" he replied with a single word: *"Perspective."*

2. **It is frequently misunderstood:** While relatively straightforward in concept, perspective is sometimes misapprehended—or at least shortchanged—in much the same way as in the parable of the blind men and the elephant (one who touches only the animal's trunk says, "An elephant is very like a snake;" Another, who feels only its leg, argues, "No, the beast is more like a tree," and so on…).

As noted at the outset, this is a *collaborative* work. The words you are reading and the images you are seeing are the product of countless hours of research, debate, and evaluation by some of Bram's most senior instructors.

In this regard, an early introduction is in order, because one of these master-teachers (Amy Kirschner) is a petite, quiet, unassuming lady, and if mention is not made of her skill and experience by others, she will be the last one to promote herself. And yet—as in many things in life—if you are not paying attention to the power of such subtlety, you are likely to miss great opportunities.

Here is an example: One evening, as the editorial team was discussing performing right-handed motions with the left hand, and at least one of their number was at risk of falling down a conceptual rabbit-hole, Amy suddenly said: *"Wait, pick up a second knife in your left hand and just parallel the motions you are doing with your right hand!"* Right-handed motions with the left hand—it was just that simple. But wait, there's more:

Amy's explanation resolved the immediate question—the *how*—but led inevitably to another—the *why*, as in, "why do right-handers need to learn left-handed motions?" Again, her explanation was straightforward and elegant: *"How you respond to an attack depends on where you find yourself in time and space. For example, circumstances will typically dictate whether you need to react on the high line or the low line in order to avoid cutting yourself. It all depends on where your arms are (opened or closed), body positioning, and so on; this will determine the defensive cut and counter. Keeping Murphy's Law in mind ("whatever can go wrong, will go wrong"), we need to learn to react with both the dominant and non-dominant hands…"*

One last thought before we move on: For any who still doubt the importance of edged tools to the evolution of the species, keep in mind that the very names of the Ages of Humanity—Stone, Bronze, Iron, and so on—refer not to the abodes in which early humans lived, the nourishment they consumed, or the manner in which they moved from place-to-place, but rather to the *tools* with which they worked in pursuit of these other necessities.

III. ORIGINS OF THE ART
The Great Wheel

In a time of rapid technological change where we have to struggle to keep up with the latest devices, apps, and operating systems, one of the appealing aspects of the practice of the martial arts is that the design of the human body—the tool with which this trade is plied—remains much the same.

Across cultures, time, and gender, almost everyone has two (and only two) arms and legs. Further, as Bram observes, those limbs are operated by mechanisms that are not much more complicated than a cable and pulley system. Accordingly, knife-fighting techniques developed and refined centuries, even millennia, ago, are still applicable and effective in the modern era.

Students of various disciplines will often debate the ultimate origin of the martial arts *ad nauseam*. Chinese emissaries, they say, brought their fighting practices to the shores of Okinawa and Japan, but before that, itinerant Indian monks traveled to China bringing with them their homeland's physical disciplines, and before that, the armies of Alexander occupied the subcontinent, no doubt introducing the occupied people to their own arts of war. So, in the end, it may be more accurate to describe the evolution of the martial arts as a circular rather than a linear process.

Images of ancient martial practices are literally carved into the rock walls of such historical monuments as the Egyptian tombs at *Beni Hasan*, and depicted in the *Knossos fresco* on the Greek island of Crete.

enhancement/detail

The Art of The Blade

PRECEPT: WHAT HAS STOOD THE TEST OF TIME?

From these ancient roots sprang many branches of blade work down through the centuries. Often, the knife was studied as an adjunct to the sword or as a minor component of empty hand practice, but in some cultures, this portable, concealable, agile weapon had entire systems developed and devoted to its proper use, and it is here that we will focus our attention.

JAPAN: *TANTO-JUTSU*

While it is certainly true that that the Japanese *tanto* was used by the *samurai* as a companion piece for the *katana* (long sword) and *wakizashi* (short sword), and also by empty-hand martial artists as an occasional tool to augment their training curricula, it should come as no surprise that in a culture where such exquisite attention is paid to detail, a variety of schools dedicated solely to this weapon arose over time.

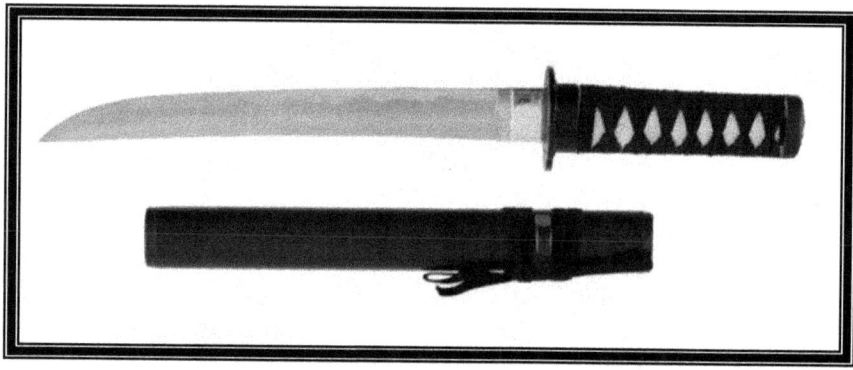

There are certainly a few blades more adept at slicing, and a handful of daggers better designed for thrusting/puncturing, but with its razor sharp edge geometry and its heavily reinforced tip, the *tanto* manages to perform both of these core functions extremely well.

PRONOUNS

Historically, many women used a version of the *tanto*, called the *kaiken*, for self-defense, but the *onna-bugeisha* (warrior women) who were part of the samurai class, learned *tantojutsu*. This text—and indeed this art—welcomes students of all genders, so when the pronoun "he" is used, it is simply for editorial convenience and old-fashioned grammatical accuracy.

ITALY: *SCHERMA DI STILETTO SICILIANO*

It is sometimes difficult to determine whether a particular school popularized a certain kind of blade, or affinity for the weapon gave rise to the school. This is certainly the case in Fifteenth Century Italy, where the stiletto was the weapon of choice and the Sicilian School of Stiletto Fighting taught people how to use it to best effect.

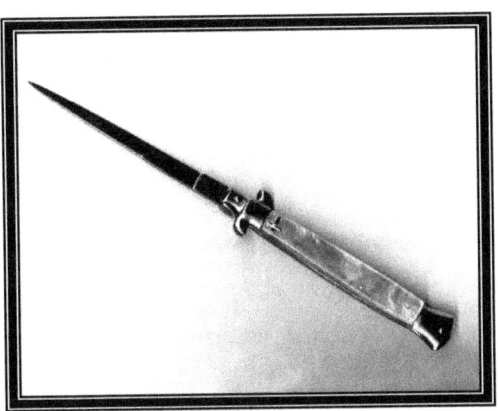

As its design suggests, the stiletto was intended primarily for thrusting. Accordingly, defensive techniques for this weapon included all manner of body shifting movements to avoid being impaled, including stepping, turning, bending, leaping and even tackling the opponent! Offensive movements primarily revolved around stabbing and then twisting on the retraction so as to inflict maximum damage.

SPAIN: *EL LEGADO ANDALUZ*

In Seventeenth Century Spain, the *navaja*—a folding knife—was a common weapon, and the correct method of use was typically passed down from father to son (and sometimes daughter) as a rite of passage.

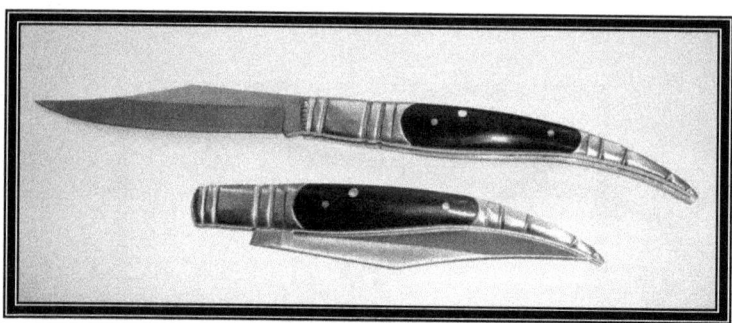

This portable, concealable weapon was a favorite among gamblers of the day, and those who studied its use favored simplified attacks and defenses based on deception, distraction, and counterstrikes.

SOUTH AMERICA: *ESGRIMA CRIOLLA*

At various times in the history of South America, the indigenous people were forbidden to wear swords (as with the subjugation of the Samurai in Japan). As a result, many took to carrying a *facón* (large knife) in their belts, typically worn transversely across the back. This weapon was a favorite of the *gaucho* of Argentina, Brazil and Uruguay, and was commonly used in conjunction with a poncho or cloak in the free hand which could be used to shield or distract.

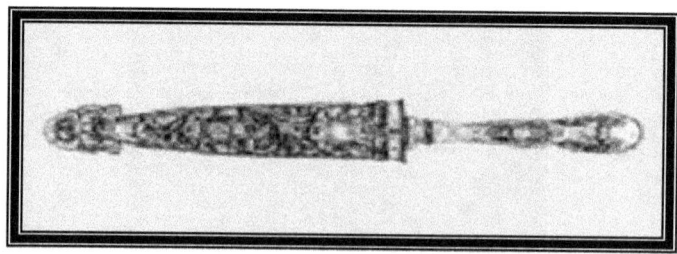

Even after the advent of firearms, this weapon remained the traditional choice for non-lethal dueling in which adversaries would slash at each other's faces until one of the combatants could no longer proceed, usually as a result of being blinded by blood.

THE PHILIPPINES: *ARNIS*

Arnis is an edged weapon (and stick) art indigenous to the Philippines. This native system of self-defense flourished for centuries in a society which very much revolved around blades, and while it is likely that European fighting methods influenced the indigenous art during the Spanish occupation from 1521 to 1898, it is noteworthy that the conquistador Magellan was killed by the Filipino warriors of *Datu Lapu-Lapu* (keep that name in mind—you'll be seeing it again) when the invading European forces first arrived on the shores of this island nation.

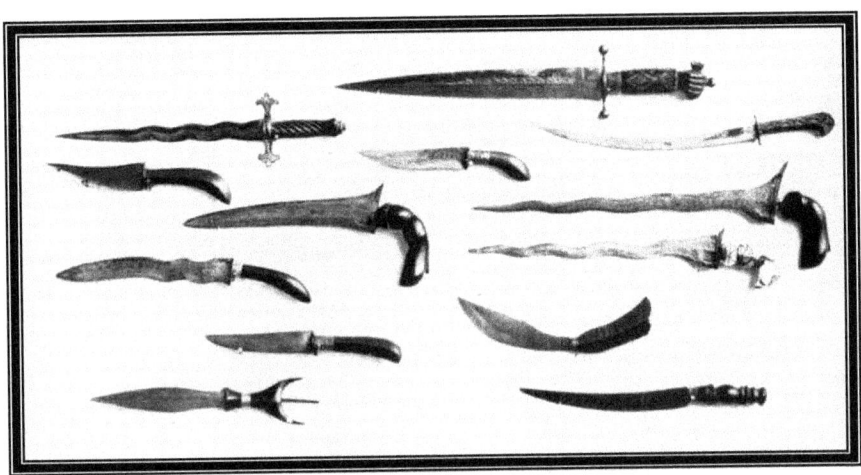

This art is characterized by constant practice, ideally involving two participants engaged in flowing 'give-and-take' drills, designed to hone physical skills and mental concentration. The most famous practitioner of this art was Remy Amador Presas—Bram Frank's teacher—and since entire chapters are devoted to these two notable individuals, no more need be written about them here.

All of which brings us to the Modern Era…

♦ JOHN RALSTON ♦
—VIRGINIA—
EVOLUTIONS: THE TOOL, THE ART, AND THE STUDENT

Bruce Lee once said: *"When I first started learning martial arts a punch was just a punch. As I progressed in the martial arts, a punch became more than a punch. And when I mastered the martial arts a punch was just a punch again."*

Just as edged tools, and the manner of their use, has evolved over centuries and millennia, so does the individual student's understanding of the art along the road from novice to master. This concept can also be expressed by the Four Stages of Competence:

1: Unconscious Incompetence—You don't know that you don't know;
2: Conscious Incompetence—You realize that you don't know;
3: Conscious Competence—You can perform when you think about it;
4: Unconscious Competence—You can perform without thinking.

Learning occurs at stages two and three. Mastery is reaching stage four. Noted contemporary of Bruce Lee and founder of *Wei Kun Do*, *Sifu* Leo Fong states: *"A beginner practices until he can do it correctly. A master practices until he cannot do it incorrectly."* Bram's take on these ideas is not unlike taking a car apart and reassembling it, not only to understand how all the parts fit together, but also to learn how they all *work* together. In this case, the car just happens to be Modern Arnis.

Many instructors employ to the K.I.S.S. method: "Keep It Simple Stupid." In Ryukyu Kempo, the corollary to this concept is expressed as the principle: Generate Confusion (a principle that matches well with one of the Ten Principles of Small Circle Jujitsu: Balance).

There are many ways to generate confusion. In fact, simply being in an altercation creates stress, which is itself a physiological means of generating confusion. This is amplified when reaching the point where you might ask, *"What do I do now?"* Most every martial artist knows this moment. You certainly do if you ever had the opportunity to learn from Professor Presas. When training with him, you likely wondered how exactly you got in the position you ended up in. And, of course, would the pain you were feeling at his slightest touch ever stop?

The way to counter such confusion is through deep understanding of your subject. Bram's approach to the martial arts is like a mechanic who takes a car apart in order to understand not just how each component works individually, but also how it all fits together. Reassembly of those parts provides simplification. And with simplification, you begin to experience **the flow**, as well as gaining a nearly subconscious understanding of how to move and counter-move…

—John Ralston

IV. THE AMERICAN TRADITION
Fighting Knives

THE GRANDDADDY

JIM BOWIE (1796-1836)

Jim Bowie (usually pronounced, "boo-ee") was a legendary American frontiersman, famed for his deadly skill with a blade. In his mid-thirties, he commissioned a knife of his own design, several variations of which went on to bear his name. Most modern Bowie knives feature a large, tough, flexible blade with a regular cross-guard and a clip point for improved control when working with the tip. A less technically precise but somewhat more colorful description is that a Bowie knife should be as long as a sword; as sharp as a razor; as strong as an axe; and as broad as an oar!

The Art of The Blade

While written records regarding Bowie's blade method are sparse, accounts of his most legendary engagement—the Vidalia Sandbar Fight—are both abundant and instructive. The year was 1827 and the place was a small sandbar in the Mississippi River near the Louisiana border, considered 'neutral ground.'

† As a threshold matter, the parties to this brawl were actually gathered in peaceful support of the two primary participants (Sam Wells and Tom Maddox) in an unrelated duel, which, ironically, ended without bloodshed.

† Bowie (a Wells supporter), however, already had bad blood with Major Norris Wright (a Maddox supporter). In fact, it was because of his ongoing feud with Wright that Bowie had resolved to carry his knife with him at all times. Wright, by contrast, was armed with a pistol.

† After the duel had ended, the two parties of supporters ran into each other again, at which point the true violence began. A good deal of gunfire was exchanged with most of the rounds missing their targets, including a point-blank shot at Bowie while he was on the ground.

† At one point in the melee, Bowie was struck in the hip by a bullet and at another, he was stabbed in the chest by a cane-sword, neither of which

injuries killed him or even prevented him from continuing—and winning—his fight against Wright by grabbing his shirt and disemboweling him with his blade.

† Following this particular engagement, Bowie was shot and stabbed again by other members of the rival party, and yet he continued to fight on, cutting off Alfred Blanchard's forearm and driving off the remainder of the Maddox contingent.

† The entire brawl lasted about a minute-an-a-half leaving two dead and two badly wounded.

These ninety seconds of violence, however, provide a lifetime's worth of lessons, including:

1. The only way to be sure you have a knife when you need one is every day carry ("EDC");

2. The threat often comes from an unexpected direction;

3. Never underestimate the power of a blade, even against a firearm;

4. Puncture wounds—whether by bullet or blade—are *not* reliable 'man-stoppers;'

5. Almost no-one truly 'wins' a fight.

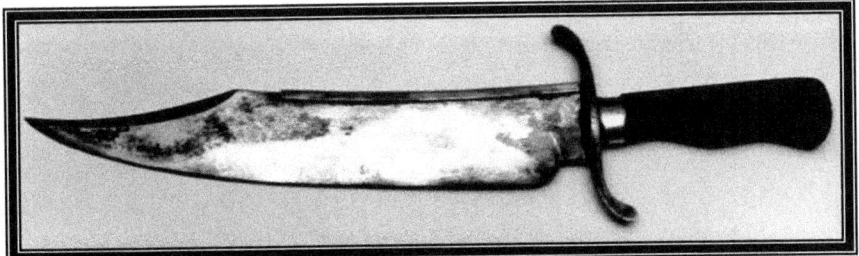

BOWIE KNIFE

THE BOWIE KNIFE

JAMES BLACK (1800-1872)

While opinions differ as to who forged the first true Bowie knife, historians generally agree that silversmith James Black—who claimed to have been the original maker—was, at a minimum, instrumental in popularizing and modifying the design.

Following a failed partnership with Arkansas blacksmith William Shaw, Black established his own forge, and at the age of 30, is reputed to have made the famous Bowie knife with which Jim Bowie killed three assassins in Texas and carried with him at the Battle of the Alamo. It is certainly clear that following Bowie's death in 1836, Black did very well manufacturing Bowie knives (behind a leather curtain to preserve the secrecy of his process) and selling them to pioneers bound for Texas.

Black lived a turbulent life, during which he was defrauded out of investments, nearly killed by his father-in-law, and mistreated by a physician, and pre-deceased by his wife. He lived out his final days in the care of friends, during which time he attempted to pass on his knife-making secrets to Daniel Webster Jones (later to become the Governor of Arkansas).

JAMES BLACK COFFIN HANDLE BOWIE KNIFE

Lumber Camps

WILLIAM WALES SCAGEL (1873-1963)

There is something very appealing to martial artists about lineage. As we reach back into the mists of time, seeking to grasp ancient knowledge, it is helpful to know whose hands it has passed through on its way to ours. And while connections are not always clear, they can often be detected by the discerning eye.

For example, William Scagel was born the year after James Black died, but there can be no doubt that as the young Scagel was learning to forge knives in the lumber camps of Canada and the Northern United States, the shadow of Bowie's famous "camp knife" loomed large on the horizon.

In keeping with another much-loved martial trope, Scagel was a bit of a recluse, leading a mostly solitary existence in the wilderness, making what he needed (including his cabin and his grinding equipment), and perfecting his art. In so doing, he revolutionized the world of blade-smithing, and genuine Scagel knives now fetch prices in the tens of thousands of dollars.

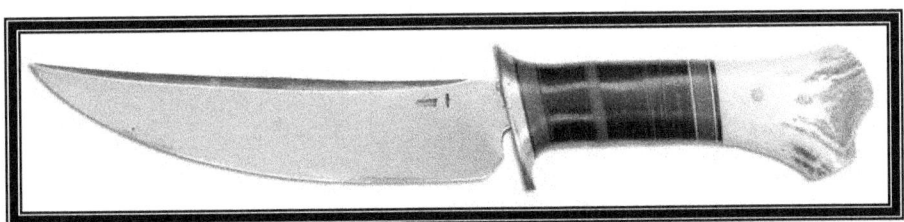

SCAGEL CAMP KNIFE (VALUED AT $40,000+)

A RUSTY HULL

WALTER "BO" RANDALL (1909-1989)

According to Bram, however, the blades which had the biggest impact on the modern fighting knife and its methods are those made by a Florida rancher-turned-smith named Walter "Bo" Randall. Epitomized by the Model 1 All Purpose Fighting Knife (to which Bram's *Abaniko* and LLC Bowie are an homage), and the Model 2 Fighting Stiletto (which Bram describes as the best dagger ever made), knives bearing the Randall name were used by many U.S. servicemen in the Second World War and beyond. Thousands were used by soldiers as a substitute for their regulation knives. They were also carried by airmen (the Model 8 Trout & Bird carried by Francis Gary Powers), Marines (the Model 14 Marine Corps Fighter), and even astronauts (the Model 17 Astro) despite space flight weight limitations.

RANDALL MODEL 1

A knife is only as good as its edge, and it would be hard to imagine a more punishing test than using it to scrape paint from the hull of a boat. This is exactly what a young Walter "Bo" Randall observed in 1936 with a knife made by William Scagel, noting with interest that following this grueling process, the blade showed no signs of damage or even wear.

Randall was so impressed with this result that he bought that very blade and subsequently began communicating with Scagel about the making process. He forged his first creation from an automobile spring and sold it to a friend, and then repeated this process, initially selling his knives one at a time.

In 1938 Randall opened a shop in Orlando, Florida, and while he initially produced blades for outdoorsmen, with the advent of the Second World War, his designs—particularly the All Purpose Fighting Knife and the Fighting Stiletto—became very popular with U.S. soldiers.

Following the War, Randall returned to the basic Bowie design for several of his combat knives, and many examples of his fine work are currently displayed at the Smithsonian Institution and in the Museum of Modern Art in New York City.

> **A GREAT RUN—THE RANDALL MADE TRADITION**
>
> **History:** As you know, my Grandfather [Bo Randall] was inspired by the work of William Scagel—that's a true story. By the time World War II came along, he had set up his own shop, and there was suddenly a huge demand from servicemen for quality knives at affordable prices. That was where his work really established its worldwide reputation. Beginning in the 1960s, he and my father [Gary] managed the business side-by-side for over twenty-five years. My brother Michael and I, in turn, worked alongside Dad for many years before he went into semi-retirement a few years ago. Randall made knives are truly a family tradition.

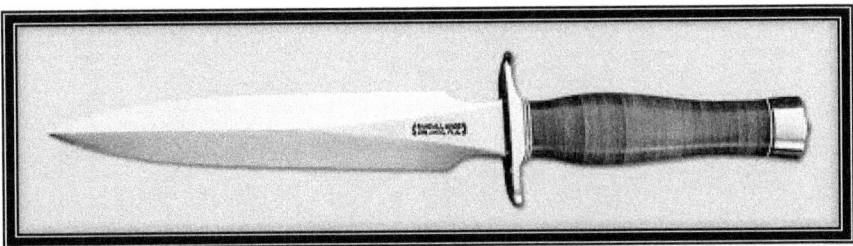

RANDALL MODEL 2

Tradition: We often see that sense of tradition among our customers as well. Generations of the same family will frequently order knives from us, and we have made and maintained some solid friendships this way. For example, we have received many letters over the years from soldiers whose lives were literally saved in combat by one of our knives, and their sons and grandsons (and daughters and granddaughters) go on to become repeat customers as well. Because demand is so high, though, there is a bit of a wait for custom orders (hopefully the knife you ordered for your daughter will be ready by the time she graduates from college)!

The Process: A lot of people debate the importance of using one particular steel versus another, but the truth is that quality knives can be made from a variety of materials. The real art lies in the process. Things like making sure not to weaken blade geometry by removing too much steel by hollowing, or taking care to produce edge material that our hard-use customers can sharpen themselves—it is these kinds of techniques that truly make the difference. We are fortunate to have a handful of skilled craftsmen in our shop who have honed their art over the course of their careers, and can turn out quality blades every time (even though no two are ever exactly the same). The only challenge is that it can be hard to make a blade that suits every customer because you just don't know what the heck they might be planning to do with it! That is why we have such a wide selection of tools in our line, each of which fits with a particular purpose.

Bram Frank: Bram has said so many positive things about our knives, and it means a great deal coming from someone who works with blades for a living. I believe I met him once when he came to visit our shop with one of his students many years ago, but I know that my father knows him well—when I mentioned his name, dad's face lit up! On behalf of the Randall family, we are grateful for Bram's kind words, and we wish him well in all his endeavors.

—Interview with Jason Randall, March 9, 2021

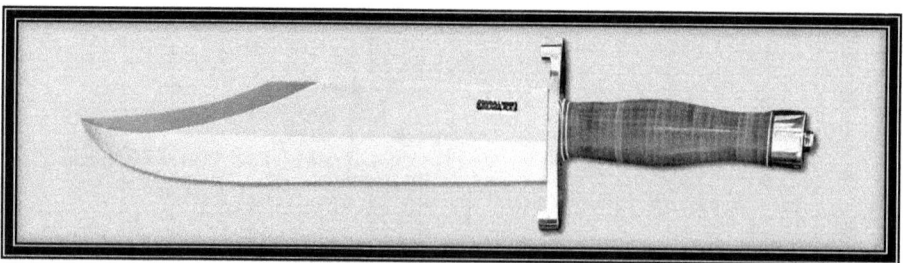

RANDALL MODEL 12

FAMOUS FOLDER

HOYT BUCK (1889-1949)

In Kansas, at the turn of the Nineteenth Century, a ten-year-old boy named Hoyt Buck became a blacksmith's apprentice and learned, among other things, how to make knives. He went on to join the Navy before the First World War and did not return to knife-making until the Second World War, when he began manufacturing "Buck" knives from worn out files in order to support the war effort.

Buck made 25 knives a week until his death in 1949, but his legacy continued through his son, Al, who began manufacturing and marketing on a much larger scale. In 1963, Buck Knives released a new model which radically changed both the trajectory of the company and the landscape of the knife manufacturing world.

The Model 110 was a folding utility and hunting knife with a sturdy locking mechanism and a substantial clip point blade suitable for butchering and skinning large game. It was one of the first lock-back folding knives considered strong enough to do the work of a fixed-blade knife, and quickly became a favorite among U.S. soldiers as an unofficial substitute for their regulation blades, making it arguably the world's first folding tactical fighter. Since its inception, fifteen million Model 110s have been sold—that's about one for every ten households in the United States.

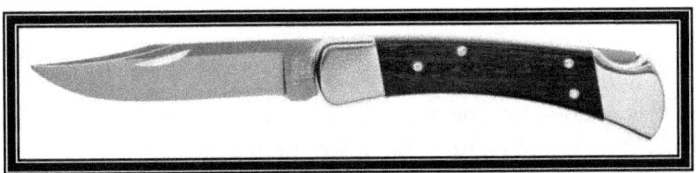

BUCK MODEL 110

PRECEPT: CHOOSE THE RIGHT TOOL FOR THE JOB.

♦ VINCE OLLER ♦

—FLORIDA—

I first met Bram Frank when we were both attending a Dan Inosanto seminar in Miami. I was with Sifu Dwight Woods of Unified Martial Art Academy ("UMAA"), another great instructor, at the time. Two things about Bram caught my attention right away: (1) He was an older gentleman who seemed to know what he was doing, and (2) he was using a Randall #1 trainer! Bram was very friendly and outgoing throughout the seminar, and was more than willing to talk to a total stranger and share his thoughts. He was anything but narcissistic, and I didn't even know that he himself was an instructor until the end of the seminar when he gave me his card and invited me to come and train with him anytime.

As it happens Guru Tony Torre, another incredible martial artist who was training with me at UMAA, was a long-time student of Bram's. This came up in casual conversation, and Tony soon became my training/sparring partner and one of my best friends. I eventually took Bram up on his offer and went to train with him. At the time he was teaching at a studio on the second floor above a Hassidic synagogue in Miami Beach—a bit of culture shock for me, I'll say!

Initially I found Bram's method a bit different from anyone else I'd ever trained with. I'd been training in traditional arts (mostly Japanese) since I was ten: Judo, Shotokan Karate, Tae Kwon Do, and so on. But through Sifu Woods, I was exposed to a whole new world of different arts: Jeet Kune Do, Wing Chun, Kali/Arnis/Eskrima, Muay Thai, the various Silats, and Savate, to name a few. My eyes were soon opened to this new range of wonderful arts.

Bram is a classic instructor—friendly but firm in class. It was obvious from the beginning that he loves what he does, and his character, knowledge and willingness to teach, all show not only his devotion, but his true love of the art. One of the things that attracted me to Bram's teachings is his love of blades. The fact that he was using a Randall #1 trainer in the seminar showed that. It also happens to be my favorite fighting knife as well. Once upon a time, I carried Randall knives in my gun shop and even had the honor of speaking to Bo Randall himself before his death. After his son, Gary, took over the family business, I happen to know that one of the people he got along with best was Bram.

Bram has a way about him, once you get to know him, he is your friend for life. He will support you, look out for you, and always have your back. Unfortunately, some people have tried to take advantage of him over the years because of this characteristic (but it never works out for them in the long run). Over the years, I have attended many seminars with Bram. In 1998, we were both at James Keating's "Riddle of Steel," a premier training camp focusing on knife skills, which was held annually at a remote location near Hells Canyon, an hour's jet boat ride down the Snake River from Clarkston, Washington. I did not even know Bram was going to be there until I ran into him on the plane in Miami! It was at this fateful camp that Bram was introduced to Sal Glesser, the owner of Spyderco Knives, launching their collaboration together on a variety of projects.

Around 2000, I was working for a large internet knife purveyor—BladeArt—and naturally turned my boss, Larry Brahms, on to Bram and his new kinetic opening tool, "the Gunting." But it wasn't until a knife show in New York that I actually got to introduce Larry to Bram, and he got to see the effectiveness of both the Gunting and the soon-to-come CRMIPT tool, as Bram used me to demonstrate them at the show.

I remember Duane Dwyer of Strider Knives ragging on me at that show for tapping out, until I asked him if he'd like to feel the ramps himself! He declined... Larry really enjoyed seeing me writhing in agony and decided he wanted to learn the way of the Gunting, so we attended the next local seminar that Bram was doing was teaching at Sensei Glen and Jody "The Gunting Goddess" Mehlman's dojo in Miami Beach.

It was at that seminar that Bram bestowed upon me a Black Belt in Combat Arnis. Foolish me, I didn't even realize what it was at first, thinking it was just a seminar certificate! He gently said, *"I think you should read it..."* It was completely unexpected, and since that time, I'm proud to say that I have earned three more degrees from him.

One of my favorite things about Bram is his love of big blades. He loves the bolos... and why not? He told me that Remy Presas once told him that he had reached the point in his training where he had to choose: The stick or the sword. Of course, Bram chose the blade.

As it happens Bram and I also share a love of certain books—the collected works of Edgar Rice Burroughs and Robert E. Howard in particular—although I'm sure there are more. To me, this is important, as reading these books as a child and young adult influenced me strongly. From my association with Bram over the years, I know they influenced him just as strongly. Integrity, skill at arms, loyalty and honor: These are the things I see in him... and by humble extension, myself. At first, neither of us realized our shared interest in these books until one day I gave him my new e-mail address and he recognized the name through its association with the cover of a particular novel. He even used this moniker on one of my black belt certificates!

Even though I have only had the privilege of meeting Bram's daughter once, we consider each other to be part of the same family, and I am so proud to be a part of his legacy.

—Vince Oller

ICEPICKS AND AWLS

A knife is a tool that separates matter. Icepick and awls are tools that puncture matter. Modular is based on biomechanical *cutting*, not *puncturing*. Even the techniques that move in a forward trajectory in this system are called 'slicing thrusts,' because they are designed to cut. This is so because—as any experienced hunter or law enforcement officer will tell you—punching holes in your target will not necessarily shut it down immediately. Biomechanical cutting will. As a result, knives and systems that are based on puncturing (stilettos and the like) are not part of this art. Theirs is another purpose, another path, and another book...

V. REMY PRESAS
Modern Arnis

Remy Amador Presas was born to Jose Presas and Lucia Amador in the tiny fishing village of Hinigaran in Negros Occidental, Philippines, on December 19, 1936.

In Tagalog, the family name is pronounced: "Preh-sas," not "Pree-sas" ("Preh-" as in "red," not "Pree-" as in "green").

Young Remy was introduced to Arnis early in life by various relatives, starting with his grandfather, Leon. This was to be the beginning of his lifelong love of the martial arts, and he proved to be a gifted and dedicated student. In his early teens, he left home to study different fighting systems and test his mettle in competition, both within and outside the ring.

At that time and place, street fights (*bakbakan*) were a common occurrence, and whenever Remy was challenged in this fashion, he regularly prevailed. In addition, he frequently entered stick-fighting tournaments that were typically held at local *fiestas*. These were full contact competitions in which the combatants did not wear armor or use padded weaponry. Because of his superior abilities, Remy always walked away with the prize money!

In 1957, at the age of twenty-one, Remy began teaching Arnis out of a small gymnasium in Bacolod City, Negros Occidental. It was here that the innovations the world would one day come to know as Modern Arnis first began to take shape. It was also during this time that he met his first wife, Rosemary Pascual, whose assistance and insights were to have a profound impact on the development of the art.

> Because Remy was functionally ambidextrous when wielding the cane, many who trained with him did not realize that he was actually left-handed—at least not until it was too late!

Beginning in 1961, the young stick-fighter studied and taught at institutes of higher learning. First at La Salle College (in Negros Occidental) and then at the University of Negros Occidental, Recoletos, he instructed classes in Shotokan Karate, Kodokan Judo, and Greco-Roman Wrestling, while at the same time pursuing his own academic studies.

UNIVERSITY OF NEGROS OCCIDENTAL (UNO) RECOLETOS

Students during these early years recall that Remy would often integrate stick-fighting techniques into his classes, even though Arnis was not, strictly speaking, part of the syllabus.

By the end of this chapter in his life, he had earned a bachelor's degree in Physical Education and senior rank in the Japanese martial arts (sixth degree in Shotokan Karate and *dan* ranking in Kodokan Judo that was to culminate at fifth degree). Interestingly, it was in the academic, rather than the martial, context that Remy first came to be called, "the Professor."

In 1969, the Presas family moved to Manila, the island nation's capital, where they rented a three-story building, the second floor of which served as a martial arts school: The National Amateur Karate Organization.

The Art of The Blade

MANILA

Why not the National Amateur *Arnis* Organization? The answer to this question lies at the very heart of the evolution of Modern Arnis: Because at that time the Filipino arts were not nearly as popular as Chinese and Japanese fighting systems, in large part because stick-related injuries were so common. One of the primary things that made Modern Arnis *modern* was the revolutionary idea that practitioners should strike stick-on-stick rather than stick-on-hand, as had previously been the custom. This seemingly simple innovation dramatically improved student recruitment and retention in an art that many characterized as 'dying' prior to the Professor's emergence on the scene. And it was this modernized version of Arnis that the Professor began layering into his classes in the Japanese martial arts.

PRECEPT: MAKE THE INNOVATION.

Studying and teaching both Japanese and Filipino systems of self-defense over the years inspired the Professor in a variety of other ways as well. For example, his creation of Modern Arnis as a discrete martial was accompanied by the adoption of a formal ranking system, specific titles, and an official uniform.

The first rank structure of Modern Arnis was as follows:
Likas (green belt)—*Likha* (brown belt)—*Lakan* (black belt)

THE ARNIS UNIFORM

In the early years of the following decade, Modern Arnis was on the rise:

✝ In 1970, the Professor created the International Modern Arnis Federation (IMAF).

✝ In that same year he gave the first of what would be several demonstrations of his art to audiences in Japan (including the police).

FILMING IN JAPAN

✝ In 1974 he authored the first book on Modern Arnis (and one of the first books about Arnis of any kind).

† In this same year, he served as the martial arts consultant on the Dean Stockwell movie: *The Pacific Connection*.

† This was also the year he immigrated to the United States in order to escape the very real danger of continuing to teach Arnis without submitting to the newly-mandated authority of the military government in such matters.

REMY AND JOSE PRESAS AT THE AIRPORT

After coming to America, the Professor continued to teach his beloved art on the seminar circuit; sometimes alone, sometimes in the company of other luminaries of the martial arts world. For many years he lived the nomadic life of an itinerant master, having no permanent address and eschewing the trappings of an anchored life. At times, the longest he stayed in any one place was during the week-long camps that were to become an educational staple for his first-generation students in North America.

NEW ENGLAND SUMMER CAMP, 1996

Intensive Modern Arnis Camps were regularly held at various venues across the United States throughout the 1990s. These martial conclaves typically lasted from several days to a week or even two. Training began right after breakfast and continued throughout the day, often lasting late into the night. Learning—both on and off the mat—occurred at a dramatically accelerated pace in this environment of total immersion, and bonds were forged that remain strong to this day. Videotaping was frowned upon, if not, banned outright: technique was expected to be absorbed organically; not frozen in a glass box. Those who were fortunate enough to attend will always remember how special these gatherings were.

† In 1982, the Professor was named Instructor of Year by *Black Belt* magazine.

† In 1994, he was selected by this same publication as the weapons instructor of the year.

The Art of The Blade

REPRODUCED WITH PERMISSION FROM *BLACK BELT MAGAZINE*

In 2000, the Professor was diagnosed with brain cancer. In February, 2001, he 'escaped' from the hospital to attend a training camp in Philadelphia. It was to be his last. On August 28 of that same year, Remy Amador Presas crossed over to the farther shore and joined the pantheon of the past masters. He was survived by his first and second wives, Rosemary Presas and Yvette Wong; his seven children, Mary Jane, Mary Ann, Remy (Junior), Maria, Demetrio, Remia and Joseph; and an extended family of friends and students all around the world.

♦ TONY TORRE ♦

—FLORIDA—

While I would undoubtedly have encountered Bram Frank eventually due to his increasing fame and our common love of the Filipino Martial Arts, the way we actually met was very reminiscent of the old adage told to us by Gautama Buddha: *"When the student is ready, the master appears."*

You see, I've been a lifelong martial artist, and at that stage of my journey, my primary martial interest was in the Filipino Martial Arts. My studies started in 1978 with Judo, and later Karate. After that, my martial journey took me through various other arts including boxing, kick boxing, Jiujitsu, Sambo, and finally (in around 1988-89), the Jun Fan martial arts which included Muay Thai and Kali-Silat in their curriculum. It was at this point that my love for the Filipino Martial Arts was firmly anchored.

Sadly, after several years of diligent training, my teacher at the time (Guro Rudy Lams the local IMB & Sayoc Kali representative) had to close his school due to some personal circumstances, and I found myself without a teacher, left with a burning desire to continue my training.

During this hiatus I euphemistically referred to my "ronin years," I continued my practice solo, and occasionally coerced others into training with me. My dear friend Bobby Sanchez (who is now a high-level martial artist in his own right) was an aspiring Wing Chun practitioner back then, and was one of those people who took the time to train with me—two beginners trying their best to get better at their chosen arts by cross training with each other was a way forward, but certainly not the most direct route (though I wouldn't trade those days for anything in world!).

The Art of The Blade

At the time, the conduit bridging our arts was our common love of boxing. It was those days that forever colored the empty hand expression of my martial arts moving forward. Arnis, however, was **gasoline** for that fire, but more on that later.

Around this time, Bobby was working at a diner in Miami Beach that was coincidentally owned by two highly skilled martial artists. It was through this relationship that Bobby met an up-and-coming, Filipino martial arts instructor named Bram Frank. He ultimately learned that Bram Frank was one of Professor Remy Presas' black belts, and his local representative. Needless to say, the news came to me very quickly, and Bobby made the arrangements for me to meet Bram.

At the time, Bram was teaching out of his home, and interviewed all of his prospective students. I immediately picked up a copy of Professor Presas' book, <u>Modern Arnis</u>, and set about memorizing it. Additionally, I dug into my library-like collection of martial arts magazines and read up on anything related to Professor Presas and Modern Arnis. These, after all, were the days before the internet was readily available. I wanted to be prepared, because any mention of an interview to me certainly meant that rejection was a possibility, and I really wanted to, "land the job."

I still remember that meeting as if it were yesterday. I was so eager to meet my new teacher that I could barely contain myself. Those that know me personally, particularly back then, know how hyperactive I can get! I made it a point to keep that in check, not wanting to turn off my potential new teacher. At the time he lived in a high-rise apartment in Miami Beach; one of those buildings that, to a simple kid from Little Havana, was where the rich people lived; heck it had 15 floors! Yes, I know, don't be too hard on me—I was young—I've lived a lot since then.

Our meeting with him went off without a hitch. I found him to be friendly and very personable, but more importantly, we had chemistry! What I thought would be a short meeting eventually became a "show and tell" of knives after he discovered I had an interest in them, and was even carrying one at the time (yes, people have been "everyday carrying" knives for a long time). This led to an impromptu training session that ran late into the evening. It was at that moment that Bram's true genius was first revealed to me. He had a deep insight into human movement and spatial relationships, but was also a graphic artist, a gourmet chef, an auto mechanic hobbyist, an EMT, a history buff, and a Mensan. All of this, along with a lifetime of martial arts, on a path similar to mine, just with an earlier start, gave him deep and rich insights into the arts and movement.

It was, however, his nuanced approach to the martial arts that gave his teaching skills such a rich flavor. He was able to decipher a person's unique style easily, and in so doing, was able to effectively prescribe the appropriate training methods to get them on the right path very quickly.

I should also mention that Bram is a very patient teacher. I came into this relationship with some previous experience, a long list of questions, and many training scars. In fact, at our first formal training session, I brought a note book to keep track of my training. Bram noticed right away, chuckled, and said, "*Right on!*"

Unlike previous martial arts I had trained in, where the student is molded to the style, Modern Arnis is very adaptable. Bram's approach, along with Modern Arnis' natural adaptability, allowed me very quickly to, "*find the art within my art*" (as Professor Presas was fond of saying).

Another phrase I started hearing a lot was: "*the flow.*" Around this time, I read the book, Flow by Mihaly Csikszentmihalyi, in which he talks about the science of optimal experience—the trance-like state where everything goes according to plan in slow motion—the 'zone,' or mental state that athletes seek to be in when looking to create optimal performances. Hearing this mentioned further reinforced the idea that I was in the right camp.

Shortly after this initial meeting, I started training privately with Bram several times a week, including the infamous 'Sunday sessions,' where I would go straight from working at a nightclub all night to training on the sandy beach which was Bram's backyard. Although I paid him by the hour, it really was by the session since he wouldn't let me leave until he was comfortable that I had digested the lesson. Sometimes (often) this took hours. He fully lived up to his goal, which was the first thing he told me before our very first training session: "*My goal is to make you better than I ever was.*" This is something I am still trying to accomplish to this day, and something I try to do for my own students.

A short time after that, Bram started teaching at Hanshi (then Sensei) Glenn Mehlman's school Beach Martial Arts. It was there that I met some of the most influential training partners of my martial career: Jody Mehlman, David Shor, and later John Ralston, many of whom you'll also meet in this book.

Along the way, I was very fortunate to have had the opportunity to participate in various winter and summer camp seminars with Professor Presas himself. Bram always prepared us well, and it was during these camps that we originally tested for rank. In fact, Bram prepared us so well that on more than one occasion, he was accused of holding us back to make himself look good (an accusation that was dispelled quickly once it was clarified that by the time of the first camp, I had only been a student of his for a little over a year)! Our training was old school "hours not years," where we practiced a lot longer, and more frequently, than the modern commonplace two-to-three hours a week.

Through those camps, and later, camps with other organizations, Bram also taught for many other great practitioners and masters, whom I had the pleasure of meeting, all of which added other parts of the puzzle for me. These included such legends as: Grandmaster Jimmy Tacosa, who was a live-in guest for a while at Bram's home; Grandmaster Wilfredo Roldan, who would occasionally teach seminars at Beach Martial Arts; Guro Doug Pierre, a common staple at the Modern Arnis camps; and many other visiting masters, such as Guro Raffy Pambuan, Grandmaster Fred Lazo, Sifu Graciela Casillas, and Master Bo Sayoc.

Ultimately, I inherited Bram's Miami Beach classes when he moved away from that area and became busy with the seminar circuit; classes which I continued to teach until a few short years ago when circumstances took me on another journey (although I still teach seminars and workshops, and may someday return to teaching regular group classes).

I have been a student of Bram's for over thirty years now, and I am glad to say that I have been a part of his journey, just as he has been the magician in my own, "hero's" journey. Along the way we became family. He has been part of my life's greatest moments, from earning my black belt in Arnis, to meeting my future wife, to the birth of my son. I've also been blessed to have met him in the early stages of his journey, so I've seen his daughter Rachel grow up and watched his knife designs go from the original paper drawings of the Escalator, to the various iterations of the Gunting, to the development of the modular system and more! But the thing that I am most grateful for is that this story continues…

—Tony Torre

VI. BRAM FRANK
A Master's Master

Those who have been fortunate enough to study at the feet of any of the true masters know that it can be challenging at times to understand exactly *what* they are doing, *how* they are doing it, or even *why* they are doing it. This is not just because they are performing at such a high degree of proficiency; it is also because they are often operating by instinct, such that *they themselves* may not even know how to explain what they are doing. This is where intermediaries—people who can translate from '*savant*-speak' to 'regular Joe' language—are so vital to the learning process.

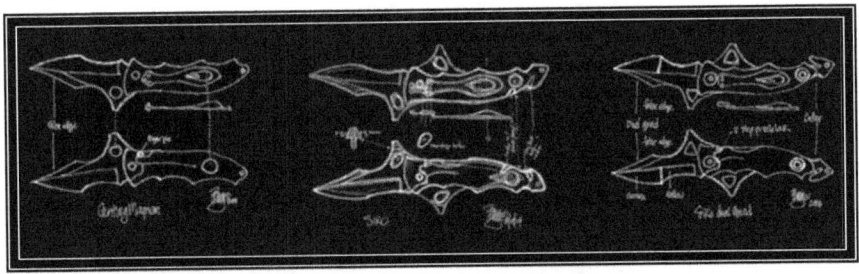

Grandmaster Bram Frank (who prefers to simply go by "Bram") is one of those rare masters who is *both* a visionary and a gifted communicator. He is able to make a knife; use it to devastating effect; and also show you how to do likewise. And much of his success as a teacher is the result of the simplicity and effectiveness of his Modular system.

Bram is a first-generation personal student of the late Grandmaster Remy Presas, the Father and Founder of Modern Arnis. He studied with Professor Presas from 1980 till his untimely demise in 2001. Bram also studied various other fighting arts such as Wing Chun, Jeet Kune Do, and American Freestyle Karate for over forty years, absorbing principles from each as they can be applied to the Filipino Martial Arts.

Bram holds *dan* rank in several arts and has been the director of blunt and edged weapons training for several federations worldwide.

† In 2004 The Senior Master Council of Modern Arnis recognized Bram as a Senior Master.

† In 2006, the International Modern Arnis Federation of the Philippines recognized Bram as Grandmaster of CSSD Conceptual Modern Arnis-Combat system, as well as an IMAFP Senior Master of Modern Arnis.

† In 2007, Bram was awarded the Gat Andres Bonifacio Award by the Philippine Classical Arnis Association in honor of his CSSD Blade systems and his dedication to the Filipino blade arts.

† In 2007, Bram was *Black Belt Magazine*'s Hall of Fame Weapons Instructor of the Year.

† In 2008, at the Fourth Filipino Martial Arts Festival, Bram was the recipient of the Lapu Lapu award, recognizing him as a Master of Blade Systems and Innovator of Blade Use and Design.

† In 2008, *Action Martial Arts Magazine* named Bram the Grandmaster of the Year and inducted him into their Martial Arts Hall of Fame.

† Also in 2008, the World Head of Family Sokeship Grandmaster Council recognized Bram with the Historical Figure Award designating him: Father of Israeli Knife Combatives. This same Council has recently recognized Bram as the first Grandmaster of a modern tactical/combative fighting art (Common Sense Self Defense/Street Combat and Modular Martial Blade Craft).

BLACK BELT MAGAZINE HALL OF FAME WEAPONS INSTRUCTOR OF THE YEAR

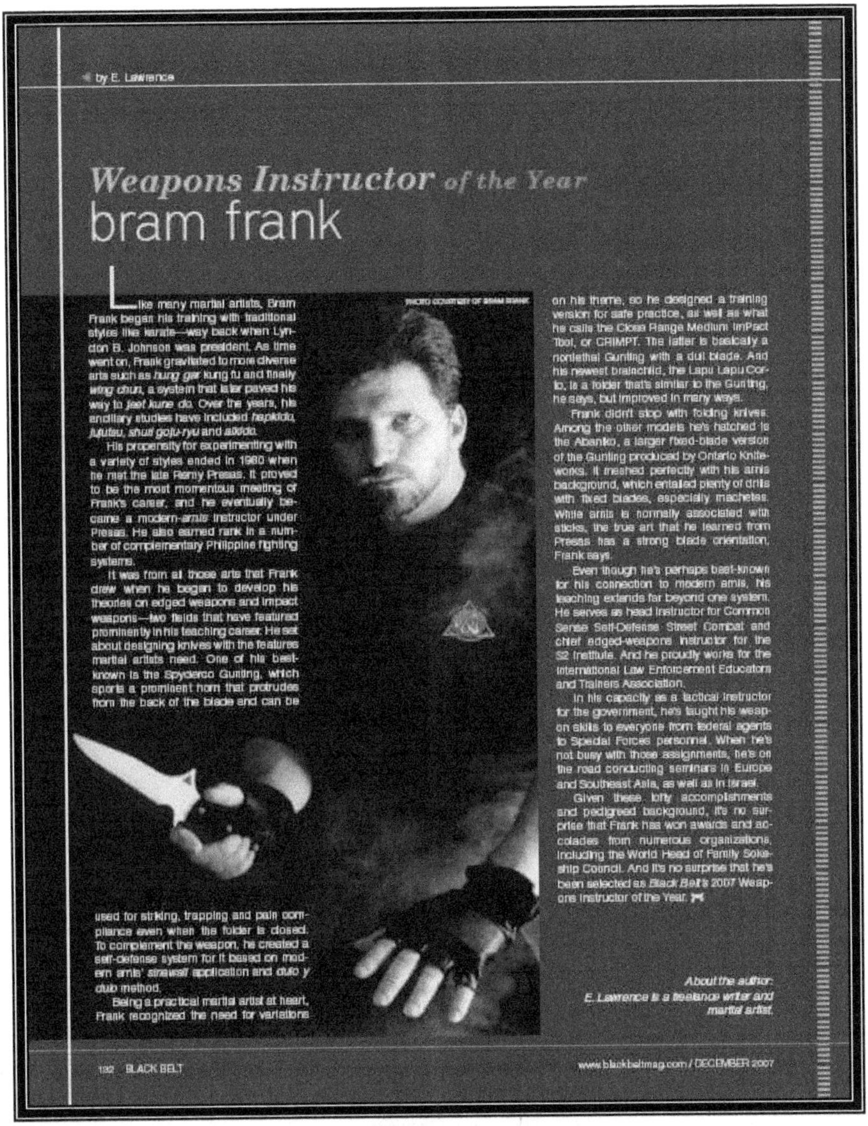

Weapons Instructor of the Year
bram frank

by E. Lawrence

Like many martial artists, Bram Frank began his training with traditional styles like karate—way back when Lyndon B. Johnson was president. As time went on, Frank gravitated to more diverse arts such as hung gar kung fu and finally wing chun, a system that later paved the way to jeet kune do. Over the years, his ancillary studies have included hapkido, jujutsu, shuai goju-ryu and aikido.

His propensity for experimenting with a variety of styles ended in 1980 when he met the late Remy Presas. It proved to be the most momentous meeting of Frank's career, and he eventually became a modern-arnis instructor under Presas. He also earned rank in a number of complementary Philippine fighting systems.

It was from all those arts that Frank drew when he began to develop his theories on edged weapons and impact weapons—two fields that have featured prominently in his teaching career. He set about designing knives with the features martial artists need. One of his best-known is the Spyderco Gunting, which sports a prominent horn that protrudes from the back of the blade and can be used for striking, trapping and pain compliance even when the folder is closed. To complement the weapon, he created a self-defense system for it based on modern arnis' sinawali application and dulo y dulo method.

Being a practical martial artist at heart, Frank recognized the need for variations on his theme, so he designed a training version for safe practice, as well as what he calls the Close Range Medium ImPact Tool, or CRIMPT. The latter is basically a nonlethal Gunting with a dull blade. And his newest brainchild, the Lapu Lapu Corto, is a folder that's similar to the Gunting, he says, but improved in many ways.

Frank didn't stop with folding knives. Among the other models he's hatched is the Abaniko, a larger fixed-blade version of the Gunting produced by Ontario Knifeworks. It meshed perfectly with his arnis background, which entailed plenty of drills with fixed blades, especially machetes. While arnis is normally associated with sticks, the true art that he learned from Presas has a strong blade orientation, Frank says.

Even though he's perhaps best-known for his connection to modern arnis, his teaching extends far beyond one system. He serves as head instructor for Common Sense Self-Defense Street Combat and chief edged-weapons instructor for the S2 Institute. And he proudly works for the International Law Enforcement Educators and Trainers Association.

In his capacity as a tactical instructor for the government, he's taught his weapon skills to everyone from federal agents to Special Forces personnel. When he's not busy with those assignments, he's on the road conducting seminars in Europe and Southeast Asia, as well as in Israel.

Given these lofty accomplishments and pedigreed background, it's no surprise that Frank has won awards and accolades from numerous organizations, including the World Head of Family Sokeship Council. And it's no surprise that he's been selected as *Black Belt*'s 2007 Weapons Instructor of the Year.

About the author:
E. Lawrence is a freelance writer and martial artist.

† In 2012, Bram was recognized by the International Modern Arnis Federation of the Philippines as a Master of the Blade in Modern Arnis and as the Guardian of the Presas Family Legacy of the Blade.

BLADE CULTURE

The Philippines is often described as a "blade culture," in large part because knives are not only commonplace in these islands, but also because, at least until recently, they have been more typical street weapons than guns. As a result, it is not surprising that this is the culture in which Modern Arnis arose.

THE INTERSECTION

What makes Bram Frank so special anyway?

Primarily this: He thinks, works, and lives at the intersection of **intelligence** and **operations**.

Intelligence—the gathering of information from all sources—is certainly a vital part of mission planning, but on occasion, those who work in this world become obsessed with amassing information for information's sake. They can become too concerned with protecting methods and sources, and therefore be reluctant to use the information they have so painstakingly collected to best effect.

Operations—the physical execution of the plan—is the way that missions are completed. Sometimes dismissed as unthinking "door-kickers," operators are the men and women who actually get the job done, but can sometimes be a little quick on the trigger (hence the jocular saying in that community: "ready, fire, aim!").

Places where these two worlds intersect are where the magic truly happens. When careful planning and subject matter expertise unite with forward pressure and strong operational tempo, the resulting momentum is unstoppable.

As a designer[2], an artist, and a really smart guy (member of Mensa and beyond), Bram has the intelligence to put it all together. As a military and police trainer[3] he has the responsibility and the operational sense to make sure that his trainees come back alive. And as anyone who works in either world can tell you, finding these two complimentary characteristics in one person is something of a rarity, and an opportunity that is not to be missed...

---

[2] <u>See</u> Appendix A—Selected Designs.
[3] <u>See</u> Appendix B—Selected Endorsements.

♦ DAN ANDERSON ♦

—OREGON—

I first met Bram in 1994. Our relationship began with Bram writing me a multi-page letter introducing himself and suggesting that all of Remy Presas's senior students should get together to catalogue his techniques. I wrote him back saying that it was a wonderful idea, but that it was never going to happen. This was not only because the Modern Arnis curriculum was about as scattered as could be—as anyone who ever attended a seminar will tell you, the Old Man didn't go from A to B to C; he went from A to 97 to π—but also because no-one could even agree about who the "senior students" were!

In our first phone call, I started the conversation by saying, "I don't know Bram Frank and I don't like him!" He cracked up and we hit it off great right from that point on. The next step happened when Bram invited me to a seminar in his home state of Florida. We were training with some of his students and Bram was demonstrating his first module, the 1-4-12 drill [often called '*sumbrada*' or 'the six-count drill' in Modern Arnis]. While many Arnisadors will defend the second strike (the lateral #4 strike) by simply dropping the cane and the check hand, I stop this strike at the elbow using my check hand. At this point, Bram goes crazy! He calls all of his students over to show them and says, *"Look! I told you that's how it's done—you stop the motion!"* And that was the true beginning of our professional relationship.

From that point on, the more I became immersed in what he was doing, the more fascinated I became by the way he took the complexity of the Filipino Martial Arts and reduced it down to pure simplicity. It was a stroke of genius, and I don't use that term lightly. And this runs in line with my own belief that the more dangerous the weapon you are using, the simpler the techniques have to be. Bram's four basic modules [1-4-12, 1-2-2, 2-3-12, and 5-2-4] cover every conceivable angle of attack using a series of simple, three-part exchanges back-and-forth.

Simple, natural movement is the key. Bram often says that almost everyone is born with two arms and two legs, and the way the typical human body functions has not changed since the beginning of time. My version of this same idea is "The Three-Mile Island Rule": Unless you were born near Three-Mile Island, all bodies are made the same so you don't need to look directly at the target in order to hit it. The head **is** on top of the neck. The knee **is** where the leg bends. Don't take your eyes off of the center mass to locate a target. Don't look at the target in order to find the target. It's where it has always been. It hasn't gone anywhere. In defending the head, unless your head is abnormally large from being born near Three Mile Island, you do not need to push the strike any more than three inches after making contact... *Four* inches if you're a chicken-guts.

Another turning point for me came when Bram sent me one of his video sets. Up until this point, my approach when dealing with a knife-wielding attacker had been to kick the weapon out of his hands (which I had successfully done in many training scenarios). This one particular tape, however, began with Bram doing what was by then to me the same old set of drills, and then, all of a sudden, the video cuts away to a shot of a denim pant leg, tied closed at both ends, hanging from a hook, with a big hunk of steak inside it.

As you know, denim is a really tough material, yet Bram makes a single pass at it with a live blade and slices out a three-inch divot! I literally jumped out of my chair and shouted out for my wife to come take a look! Having seen this, the idea proposed by some karate fighters that they would be willing to take a cut in order to deliver a blow, turned 180 degrees for me. And ever since then, I've worked Bram's material and integrated it into what I do. I have even written a book about this integration: <u>Steel Meets Flesh-Modular Knife Fighting Transitioned To Empty Hand Applications</u>.

I always tell Bram that I am a 'banger,' not a 'cutter' (to which he always replies, *"No young man, you are a cutter…"*). But here's the thing: Cutting someone with a blade has a certain emotional content—which I don't have—and it also triggers serious legal consequences. As a result, I don't carry a knife. But even though knife-fighting is not a huge part of what I practice and teach on a regular basis, I truly believe that in order to be able to defend against a weapon, you also need to know how to use it, and it is for this reason that I pay so much attention to what Bram teaches.

> Remy Presas—both Bram's and my teacher—taught different things to different people along the way. For example, almost no-one ever saw him talk about Tai Chi Pushing-Hands, but I have video of him performing it with me—he just inserted it in the middle of a six-count drill! It just depended on where you caught him at any given time. The reason that Bram learned so much about the role of the blade in Modern Arnis is because he is the one who pestered Remy about it the most! To get this piece of the Modern Arnis puzzle, Bram is the only guy to go to.
>
> And as a human being, Bram is entirely consistent. If you didn't like him twenty years ago, you're not going to like him now. But the reverse is also true. And despite what I said when I answered that first phone call over a quarter of a century ago, I like Bram!
>
> —Dan Anderson

Bram is currently the Director of Edged Weapons training at the S2 Law Enforcement-Security Institute. Over the past several years Bram has concentrated on the use of edged weapons/tools as principal instruments of self-defense and has focused on their military, law enforcement, and counter-terrorism applications.

PRECEPT: TEST YOUR ART IN THE REAL WORLD.

VII. TOOL OF CHOICE
The Lapu-Lapu Corto (LLC)

The selection of a blade depends entirely on what its intended use will be. While the outdoorsman and the soldier may be looking for a multi-purpose tool that can hammer a nail, open a can, and stab an enemy, for the civilian interested in every day carry ("EDC") for self-defense purposes, there will be a very different set of criteria, including such considerations as: Legality, concealability, ease of deployment and use, force escalation capability, retention characteristics, and even alternate functionality.

With these imperatives in mind, it should come as no surprise that the tool of choice here is one of Bram Frank's blades—tools specifically designed for use with the Modular system—and in particular, the *Lapu-Lapu Corto*.

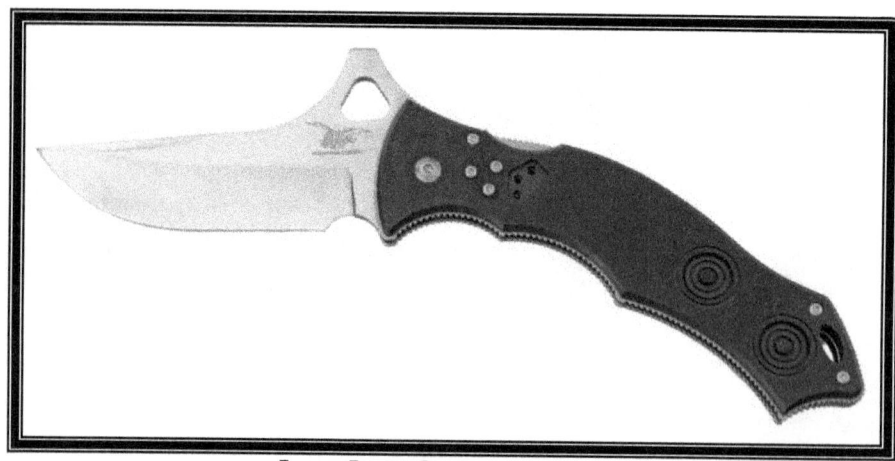

LAPU-LAPU CORTO—BOWIE

✦— Over the past quarter century, many of Bram's knife designs have fallen into what he calls, "the *Gunting* Family" (named after a scissoring action common to the FMA), of which there are various different 'members." Before examining the individual variations, however, it is important to understand the characteristics that are common to them all:

1. A Relatively Short, Broad Blade: The compact size of these blades—particularly the three inch 'Standard' as opposed to the four inch 'Magnum'—makes them easier to carry and conceal, harder to trap, and *likelier* not to run afoul of various knife length laws (which vary from jurisdiction to jurisdiction but are commonly around three inches). At the same time, because of the way in which these knives are used in the Modular system, this length is sufficient to perform all techniques.

2. Indexing: These depressions and protrusions in the handle and clip are designed to allow for tactile orientation and controlled grip transitioning;

3. Ergonomics: The pistol grip—in combination with other ergonomic aspects of the tool's design—enables powerful, intuitive, gross-motor, grabbing and gripping using the web of the hand and also parallels firearm lock activation/visual confirmation;

4. The Raised 'Dorsal Fin' Ramp (the so-called "Bramp") [δ]: This feature allows the tool to be used as an impact weapon for pressure point striking and a flesh or fabric grabber when closed and also enables kinetic opening using parts of the opponent's body (or even, with care, the practitioner's);

5. The 'Teeth': This 'jimping' on the ramp, the lock-release, and elsewhere facilitate the grabbing and trapping of flesh and cloth;

6. The 'Horns': These outcroppings at various points on the profile are also designed to facilitate grabbing and trapping flesh and cloth;

✦— In addition to offering a choice of sizes and styles, some of Bram's blades are available in fixed configurations. Unless you live in a place where the sight of a knife sheath on a belt is common, you will probably want to choose a folder for EDC, which gives rise to certain additional features:

7. The Puzzle Lock: This mechanism ensures that once locked open, the tool will not close accidentally;

8. The Ambidextrous Clip: This feature allows the tool to be oriented comfortably according to personal preference and varying hand dominance; serves as an additional indexing point; *and*, because of its visibility, reduces the chances that it will be treated as 'concealed';

The Art of The Blade

✝ Certain members of the *Gunting* Family (more fully illustrated in Appendix A, page 218) bring additional specialized features to the table, such as:

9. Seat-belt Cutter/Window-breaker: While not common to all of Bram's designs, these specialized features have myriad uses over and above those for which they are ostensibly intended;

10. Blade Shapes[s]: Each of the following available blade shapes has its own, unique capabilities, such as the recurved edge's ability to 'grab' and control the item being cut. All of them, however, can be used to perform Filipino fighting techniques including cutting, thrusting, tip ripping, and tip leading cuts.

From left to right:

✝ Bram Bowie;

✝ Persain [sic];

✝ Gunting Spearpoint;

✝ LLC *Katana*;

✝ Reverse Tano/SIS Christian;

✝ RAF-2 Dagger;

✝ Tactical *Tanto*; and

✝ *Khopesh*.

♦ Dave Giddings ♦

—Florida—

Ironically enough, even though we both live in Florida, I first met Grandmaster Bram Frank in the Philippines. I went to attend the Filipino Martial Arts ("FMA") World Festival, which occurs every two years, and there was Bram. Even though we had just met, he was very cordial and invited me to join his group. He is a very giving person and is always open to sharing his knowledge with anyone who is sincerely interested. I have been with Bram ever since and I am grateful for his mentorship and friendship.

I'd like to discuss the terminology and the various meanings and uses of the word: *"gunting."* *Gunting* in Tagalog means, "scissors." In FMA, we use the term to describe a scissoring action, but Bram has also designed a knife called, "the Gunting," which debuted in the year 2000. Bram's current LLC Gunting models are the evolution of this design concept. We'll talk first about the *gunting* motion itself and then about the Gunting knife.

A *gunting* movement can be performed in various ways. It can be done both horizontally and vertically. It can be performed with the empty hands, with a *dulo-dulo* (palm stick), with a *baston* (cane), and with a blade. Virtually all FMA systems include this movement in some form. Since Bram is, as Professor Remy A. Presas described him, *"the man with the knife,"* naturally his focus is on the blade.

The *gunting* action is typically used to simultaneously defend against the opponent's attack while also attacking the opponent's limb. This concept embodies the Filipino principal of, *"defanging the snake"*. As previously mentioned, this motion can also be performed with empty hands, a *dulo-dulo*, or a *baston*. When performed with empty hands (or a *dulo-dulo*), there is plenty of space to work with. With the *baston* there is less space. With all of the non-bladed applications, there is no danger of the crossing hands and being cut, but with the blade, this is a serious issue.

The *gunting* movement is used in many of Bram's core modules. Because of the nature of bladed engagements, Bram stresses a couple of key concepts, including edge awareness and body shifting, in order to allow for *gunting* to be performed safely.

Live Hand In Front: For example, let's use a common horizontal split-entry *gunting* motion against a Modern Arnis Angle #1 strike (or a simple straight right-hand attack) as a template for our discussion. In this example, the defender has a blade in his right hand. The defender's right hand is inside the opponent's right-handed attack and the defender's empty hand (live hand) is outside the opponent's attacking limb. If the defender's live hand is even with, or in front of (closer to the attacker), the bladed hand, he may cut himself if he performs the *gunting* motion.

If the defender shifts his body to the right, however, he will create the space needed to be able to perform the *gunting* motion safely. The defender can check with the live hand near the opponent's elbow and draw the blade back to cut the opponent near the wrist, with sufficient distance between the hands to ensure that they won't cross. The defender's blade is now above the live hand and he can freely counter-attack using the high angle. In this way, body shifting creates the space needed to allow the hand positions to alternate safely.

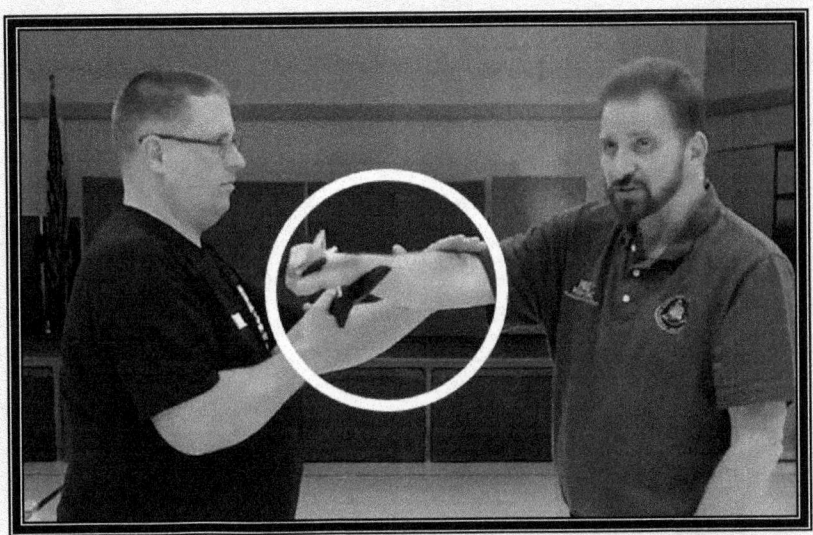

Live Hand Behind: Using the same split-entry template as the previous example, if the defender's live hand is behind (further from the attacker) the bladed hand, he can still safely perform the *gunting* motion. From there, he will be free to counter with a mid or low angle attack. He will, however, face a similar problem if he tries to withdraw the blade and counter with a high angle attack. Although he can move the blade underneath the other limb, it will be easy for the opponent to check the live hand/arm downward and he will likely be cut. The defender's blade will still be in front (closer to the attacker) of the live hand, so the defender can pick the blade up and execute an *abaniko* (fanning) movement while body shifting to the right to safely pass the attacker's arm over to the defender's right.

This will allow the defender's live hand to be safely re-inserted in order to check the opponent's arm and the defender can then counter with a high angle attack without crossing his arms and risking being cut. Again, edge awareness and body shifting allows for the safe alternating of the hand positions.

This may seem elementary to some people, but I often see students crossing their hands like this when performing these types of movements with empty hands or impact weapons. As Bram likes to say, *"As you train, so shall you do."* If you don't focus on edge awareness when training these motions, you will likely cross your hands and be cut when using a blade, especially at high speed and under duress. Using the blade is different than using impact weapons. I can assure you Bram is not being pedantic about this. Being too nonchalant about edge orientation will result in bad things happening.

The other side of this *gunting* discussion is the Gunting knife itself. Bram's LLC (*Lapu-Lapu Corto*) Gunting knife comes in three primary configurations:

(1) A blunted training drone (color-coded **red**);

(2) A non-sharp-edged working tool (color-coded **blue**); [the CRMIPT—for first responders]

(3) A live blade with a sharp edge (commonly color-coded **black**, but also **any color other than red or blue** (tan, camouflage…).

The LLC Gunting can be used to disable an opponent by striking and/or controlling limbs while targeting various non-lethal pressure points on the opponent's body with the weapon, either open or closed. The first feature you will notice (common to all three designs) is the ramp, or 'Bramp', on the blade. This ingenious shape allows the user to perform a variety of techniques, two of which are especially applicable to the *gunting* motion:

(1) In the closed position, the ramp allows for the striking of the opponent's limbs.

(2) The ramp also allows for kinetic opening of the blade by leveraging it against the opponent.

When combined, the user can perform *gunting* using the tool as an impact weapon and then roll straight into a kinetic opening, which allows the user to escalate to cutting with the blade as needed.

In this way, the LLC Gunting embodies another key concept which Bram espouses: Escalation of force. Using *gunting* motions, the practitioner can work his way up the opponent's anatomy, progressing from biomechanical stoppages (like cutting tendons and muscles for limb destructions) all the way up to severing vital components if—and only if—extreme circumstances warrant it. Such actions are, of course, not to be taken lightly. The ability to escalate force as needed allows the well-trained user to employ just enough force to stop the attacker and no more. The LLC Gunting knife design embodies this concept and provides the user with the ability to employ less-than-lethal techniques (such as pressure point controls using the ramp, scales, or butt), while at the same time keeping lethal force options in reserve if needed. This is what truly makes the LLC Gunting so different from all other knife designs.

My hope is that this discussion of *gunting*—both the tool and the motion—has provided a helpful glimpse into Bram's approach to Professor Presas' art. Bram's perspective on this subject is truly unique, as is manifest in both his innovative blade system and in his amazing knife designs. I, for one, believe that these are very important contributions to the Filipino Martial Arts.

—Dave Giddings

| Precept: It's Hard to Beat A Tool Purpose Built for the Job at Hand. |

11. Legality: The way in which a tool comports (or doesn't) with the legal requirements in your jurisdiction is of paramount importance. Knife laws vary widely from place-to-place, and are often in flux, so it would be foolish to try to provide an exhaustive analysis in this forum, but the following are some common factors that should be taken into consideration when trying to determine what might be an appropriate EDC tool.

The switchblade and the *balisong* are probably the two most vilified knives in the bladed armamentarium. This is partly the result of bad press and partly because they can be opened in a single-handed manner, which many legislators believe is indicative of intent to employ them combatively.

Whether or not you agree with this assessment, mere possession of these weapons is illegal in some places, and is heavily regulated in most. If you own either—or any other kind of blade which can be opened using just one hand—you'd be smart to check the specific law of your jurisdiction, especially before taking it outside of your home.

COMMON FACTORS

Mechanism: Even though Bram's patented kinetic opening mechanism can be used one-handed, it doesn't *seem* like it should fall into the catch-all "mechanical or gravity-assisted" description common to most restrictive knife laws. It is, however, still worth keeping this regulatory factor in mind.

Blade Length: Another way of regulating knives is based on blade length. While this varies from place to place, under three inches is a common 'safe harbor' length, in part because law-makers suppose (probably incorrectly) that less harm can be inflicted with a shorter blade. Some of Bram's designs fall under the critical "cut-off" length; others do not. In this regard, it is important to choose the right tool for the job.

Concealment: Perhaps the most important factor in the criminal context is whether the weapon is concealed—which, depending on how the law is written and interpreted—can mean *either* hidden on your person *or* carried in a car where it is not in plain view. The clear preference is for visibility, which leads to the odd result that walking down the street holding an assault rifle (with all the apprehension that will likely cause) may be legally safer than carrying a knife in your pocket.

Purpose: In some cases, mere possession of a certain type of weapon (like a switchblade) is illegal. In others, it matters *why* you are carrying that particular item. In Pennsylvania, for example, almost anything can be considered "an instrument of crime," if it is carried with the intent to use it for an unlawful purpose, and that intent will be inferred from the specific circumstances that apply in a given situation.

Status: Finally, the status of the person carrying the weapon is often determinative. For example, most jurisdictions have exceptions to weapons regulations for law enforcement officers and members of the military. In this regard, your status as a martial artist may also be a benefit in the sense that you have a legitimate reason for carrying a weapon if it is truly for training purposes (but you better be on your way to or from class).

The Art of The Blade

VIII. CHOOSE YOUR SYSTEM
Modular Knife Combat/Concepts

As advertised at the outset, this book is not only biased toward **Bram Frank's Modular** system; it was specifically written to commend this excellent method to your attention, and to help you take your first few steps along this particular way. This is so because Modular has several elements that are uniquely sensible and effective, both individually, and as part of the larger program.

Modular: The term "modular" simply means that system is broken down into discrete, standalone pieces, each of which can be learned separately and later combined into various cohesive patterns. Or as Bram succinctly explains: *"It's like a Lego set."*

As threshold matter, a distinction should be made between knife self-defense and knife-fighting. In the former scenario, the practitioner is usually empty-handed, whereas in the latter, both parties are typically armed. Accordingly, the tactics, techniques, and imperatives are markedly different. While many schools of martial arts purport to teach at least some rudimentary knife self-defense, very few focus on the practicalities of knife-fighting, and even fewer do so with the benefit of real-world testing. Having spent a lifetime designing, making, and testing blades; having learned at the feet of past masters for years; and having taught his art to combat professionals the world over for decades, the architect of the Modular System has truly been "there" and done "that".

PRINCIPLE: ENSURE ACCESS TO YOUR BLADE

Ensure Access: The best knife in the world is useless if you can't reach it; keep your blade accessible at all times. In your home, this simply requires keeping track of the tool at all times—a practice that falls squarely within the realm of good common sense. For those who are new to blade-work, rapid acclimatization to this new normal can be had by following the old martial tradition of taking the new weapon with them everywhere they go for a week or so.

But outside the home, in modern society, this is a lot easier said than done. Gone are the days when a frontiersman could walk around town with a Bowie knife strapped to his hip without generating unwanted scrutiny and perhaps undue alarm. Even the tell-tale glint of a clip on the belt will catch and hold the attention of interested onlookers—just watch the gaze of any law enforcement officer who sees this in a public setting. This, then, is the first of many features of the Modular system which recommend the adoption of this method.

In addition to his many excellent fixed-blade knives, Bram makes a variety of complimentary folding knives, each of which locks immovably into place with his patented puzzle mechanism. As a result, the user of blades made for specifically for the Modular system has access to a variety of powerful tools which can be easily and safely concealed in a pocket, making every day carry ("EDC") a realistic endeavor. And while statutes vary from jurisdiction to jurisdiction, the relatively short, stout blade of Bram's folders tends to fall on the right side of the law, while still being sufficient to get any job done.

Finally, Bram's folding knives are specifically designed to execute Arnis-style techniques, like the scissoring motion known as *'gunting'* (from which one of his most popular blades takes its name) when open, but also to serve as an effective striking (Bramp) and grabbing (jimping) tool when closed.

THUMBS UP!

Like many masters, if you *watch* what Bram is doing while teaching (as well as *listening* to what he is saying), you will pick up some hidden gems along the way.

For example, when discussing a particular blade technique, he will sometimes demonstrate with his empty hands, extending the thumb of one and pulling back the palm of the other to his chest while doing so. There are major implications to be gleaned from these seemingly minor movements:

i. The extended thumb provides visual confirmation of blade orientation (up for forward grip and down for reverse) when instructing;

ii. The retracted hand is indexed on the chest in order to keep it away from the field of blade engagement until and unless it is intentionally deployed (note how this posture is reminiscent of the Modern Arnis courtesy) [𝄞];

iii. The elbows/forearms are positioned and employed as feelers (as Bram puts it: *"Like a second set of hands"*) in a posture known as "wedging in."

Familiarity with this posture ensures that students will always have what is needed to practice edged tool techniques "on hand," even in situations where a trainer drone is not available or a knife is not allowed; the specific hand positions reinforce safe training methods; and the overall practice exemplifies the interchangeability of tools and empty hands; a feature that lies at the core of many of the Filipino Martial Arts.

PRINCIPLE: DO NO HARM

Habit Consistency: The only thing worse than being cut by an adversary is cutting yourself. For this reason, the Modular system stresses the importance of safety first, teaching students to keep their empty hands as far from the cutting zone as is operationally practical. More than this, because performance under stress is dictated by past practice, it is *vital* to pay due attention to habit consistency—the process by which hundreds and thousands of repetitions of a given movement in the *dojo* will indelibly engrave the pattern of the technique on the nerves and musculature of the practitioner. If you are 'cutting' yourself in practice, you can be pretty sure you will cut yourself as badly—or worse— 'in real' (as Remy used to say).

FORGED IN FIRE
Forged in Fire is a History Channel series in which skilled contestants compete to forge a variety of edged weapons, and a panel of expert judges then subjects the finished weapons to a series of punishing tests. In its eighth season at the time of this writing, it is fair to say that the judges on this show know a thing or two about swinging a blade safely. And it is instructive to note that the way in which they routinely index the free hand on the chest when cutting is highly reminiscent of the Modern Arnis salutation…

Color Coding [η]: In addition to teaching safe technique, Bram also employs a color-coded safety system in manufacturing his wide array of products: Red for training 'drones,' blue for blunt working tools (see the Chapter on the less-than-lethal approach); and black for live blades.

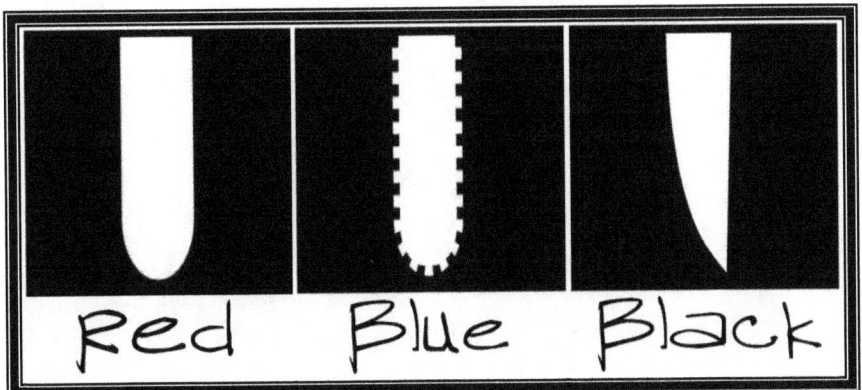

The Puzzle Lock [θ]: A major factor in "doing no harm" with a blade—particularly when using a folding knife—is making sure it does not accidentally snap shut on your own fingers (or fail to lock open) when being deployed. Fortunately, Bram has designed and patented a system known as a "puzzle lock," which renders this all-too-commonly self-inflicted injury in the blade world a virtual impossibility.

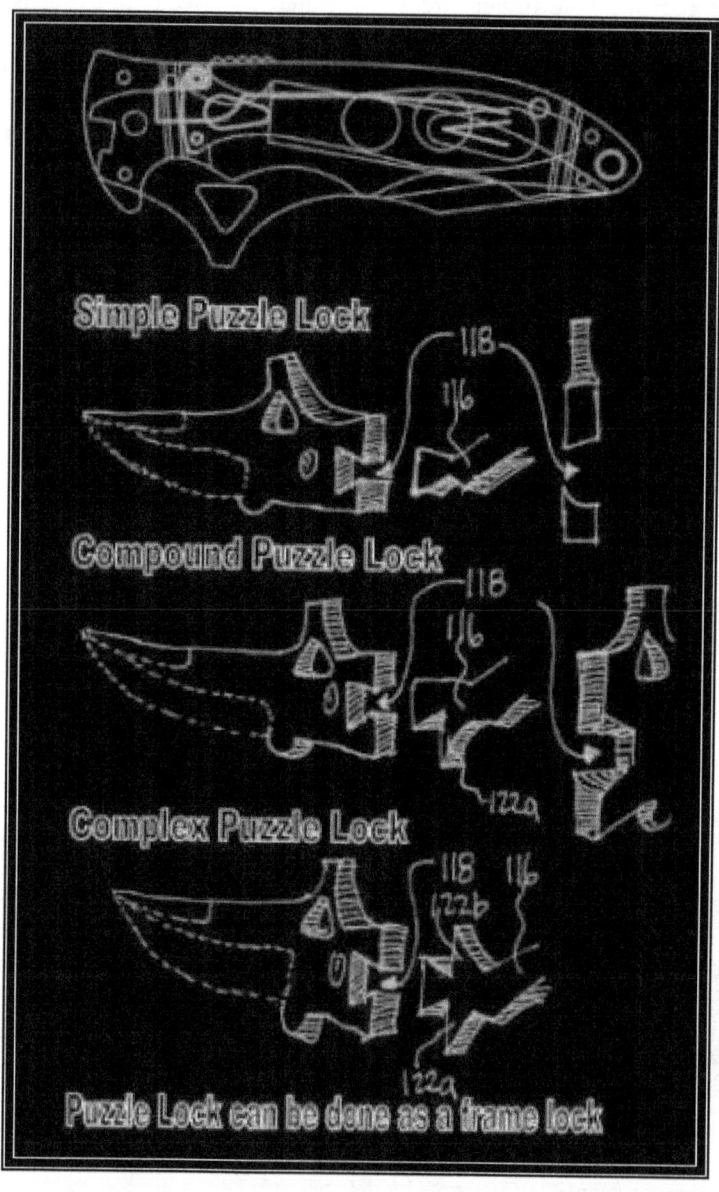

Principle: Cut (and Block) Correctly

The Art of the Cut [*t*]: As any chef knows, a knife cuts by making contact and then drawing through. Why, then, do so many students and teachers use this elegant tool to hack, stab, and chop, when the instrument is specifically designed to slice? Students of the Modular method are taught to practice executing this critical motion by carving clean a succession of slices from the end of cylindrical foam floats, which approximate the consistency of flesh and can add 'bone' to the exercise by inserting a PVC pipe into the hollow core. Once the importance of this fundamental movement has been truly grasped, the practitioner will never slice another shipping box, length of fabric, or hearty sandwich without thinking of this technique.

Gross Motor/Natural Body Movement: Almost all students and teachers of the blade agree that body movement is essential to the art. From stepping/shifting to move the target out of range to striking with the force of the hip, the body is an essential—if often overlooked—component of solid technique. However, both institutional studies and common experience confirm that the stress associated with violent encounters dramatically inhibits the body's ability to perform. Accordingly, the techniques of the Modular system are based on the body's natural reactions and gross motor movements. While there is no guarantee that these types of actions will be impervious to the fog of war, they will generally be the last to go.

THE NATURAL LAW

It is essential to note that the basic moves in Modular mimic the body's natural gross motor skill survival responses of:

1. Protecting the head/face on the high line;
2. Protecting the abdomen on the low line; and
3. Covering the top of head and core on the vertical line.

As Bram teaches all new students, the human body is only capable of moving in certain ways—the design has not changed much over the millennia. When it comes to an arm, it can either be open or closed. That's it. There are no other choices. Open or closed.

Since most people have two arms, however, the open-closed proposition can be extended to encompass all possible movement combinations:

1. Following: One arm opens, the other arms opens; one arm closes, the other arm closes...

2. Alternating: One arm opens, the other arms closes; one arm closes, the other arm opens.

3. Weaving: As in *Sinawali*

[These foundational concepts are well illustrated in the "Gross Motor Skills" clip on Bram's pivotshare site]

Again, according to Bram, that's it—these options are carved in stone. When broken down this way, the chaos of combat, in which seemingly almost anything can happen, starts to take on a discernable pattern—a pattern with which we can work...

Using this model, we can, for example, inject the following *additional descriptors* into the foundational 1-4-12 pattern (illustrated in Chapter X):

1. *Open to closed* on a high-to-low diagonal (#1 strike);
2. *Recover from closed to open* on a horizontal plane (#4);
3. Downward vertical (#12).

The distinction between open and closed becomes especially important when assessing defensive options to the same strike. For example, an "open #2" response may differ markedly from a "closed #2" response.

Bio-mechanical Function [x]: Anybody who has seen combat or worked as a medical first responder (as has the designer of the Modular system) knows that those injured by gunshots or puncture wounds often exhibit a surprising degree of resiliency and can sometimes continue to walk, talk, and fight hours after such damage has been inflicted on them. Even massive amounts of blood loss ('the hydraulic system' in Bram-speak) will not reliably shut someone down. The limbs, by contrast, absolutely and immediately cease to function the instant that the nerves, tendons, and joints ('switches,' 'cables,' and 'pulleys' in Bram-speak) which control them are severed. It is like having an 'off switch' for the offending limb.

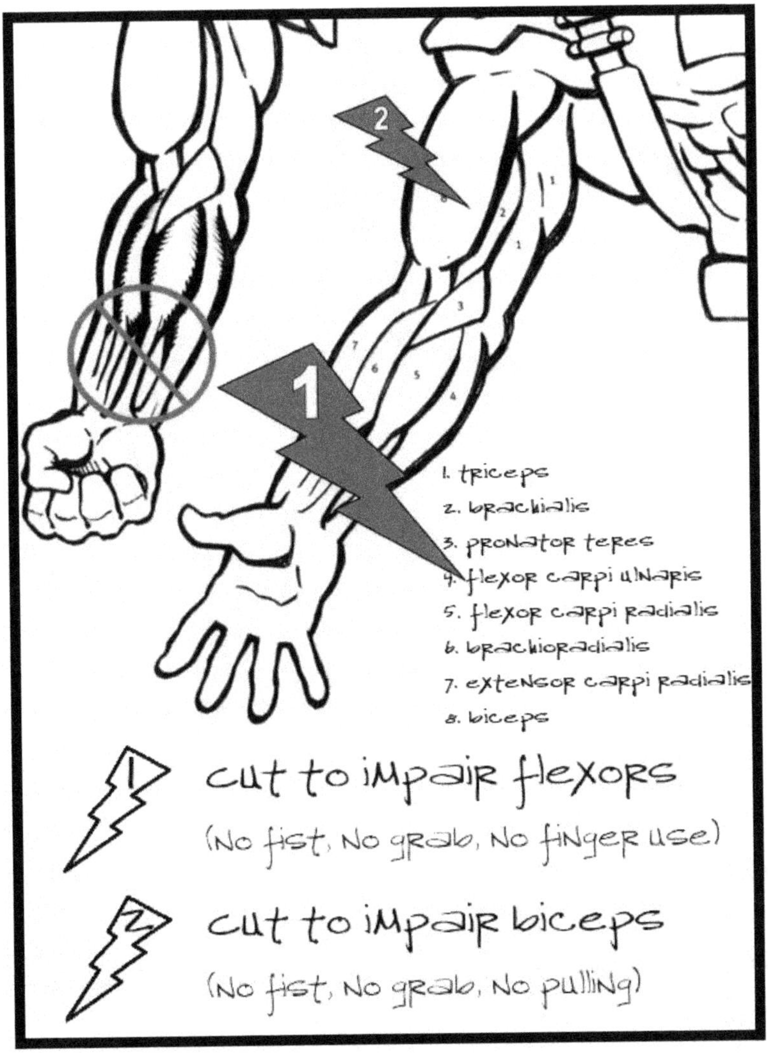

1. triceps
2. brachialis
3. pronator teres
4. flexor carpi ulnaris
5. flexor carpi radialis
6. brachioradialis
7. extensor carpi radialis
8. biceps

cut to impair flexors
(No fist, No grab, No finger use)

cut to impair biceps
(No fist, No grab, No pulling)

Intent: Because of the rhythmic and collaborative nature of give-and-take drills, there is a danger that practitioners can be lulled into treating it as playing patty-cake. While this kind of approach may help to learn the approximate movements, without realistic intent, it creates nothing more than a Hollywood façade. When practicing in earnest, it is important to remember that a real world opponent will be *trying to kill or maim you*, and you are quite literally fighting for your life. Consequently, while maintaining appropriate training courtesy, remember not to move politely around your opponent, but rather *displace* him (or her) as needed.

According to Bram, each defensive physical maneuver must be built around a specific tactical goal and performed with a combat mindset:

#1/#2: As in JKD, you must **intercept and attack** these strikes;

#3/#4: You must **close range and fully commit**.

#5: Displace the body first; the blade technique is only **insurance**.

#12: The **earlier you intercept** this attack, the more effective.

Targeting: It is important not to confuse angles with targets. *Angles* (see Chapter XIII) refer to the blade's trajectory, regardless of what part of the opponent may be in the line of fire depending on position and posture. *Targets*, by contrast, are the anatomical structures the practitioner aims for by choosing the right angle for the idiosyncrasies of any particular engagement.

In the chart that appears on the following page, common Modular targets are enumerated and simplified analysis provided in the following categories:

1. **Access:** How easy or hard is it to reach this target and at what range?

2. **Armor:** How much bone or thick muscle protects the target?

3. **Mechanical:** How bio-mechanically effective will damage be?

4. **Hydraulic:** All cuts will bleed, but is this a blood-supply-rich target?

5. **Electrical:** All cuts hurt, but is this a nerve-heavy region?

6. **Other:** Are there any special considerations (like percussion)?

Bone Barrier: The corollary to cutting correctly is blocking correctly. In the heat of battle, the best laid plans often fall apart: Weapons are dropped; strikes miss their targets; and blocks collapse. And when working with edged tools, the first failed block is often the last one as well. As a result, Modular blocks are either blade-to-flesh or bone-to-bone. By using the two strong bones of the forearm to perform the latter, Bram's blocks (unlike those which use fingers, wrists, or hands) are virtually impenetrable.

The Art of The Blade

TARGETS

Target	Access	Armor	Mechanical	Hydraulic	Electrical	Other
Fingers/Thumb	Easy/far	Moderate	High	High	High	High shock; slippery
Carpus (wrist)	Easy/far	Minimal	High	High	High	Ideal Intercept
Outer Forearm	Easy/mid	Moderate	High	Low	Moderate	Hand extensors
Inner Forearm	Easy/mid	Minimal	High	High	Moderate	Hand flexors
Elbow joint	Easy/mid	Moderate	High	Minimal	High	Percussion
Biceps	Easy/close	Moderate	Moderate	Moderate	Moderate	Forearm flexors
Triceps	Situational	Moderate	Moderate	Moderate	Moderate	Forearm extensors
Deltoid	Moderate	Moderate	High	Moderate	Moderate	Arm rotate/extends
Pectorals	Easy/close	Moderate	Moderate	Moderate	Minimal	Arm adduct/rotation
Trapezius	Easy/close	Moderate	High	Moderate	Moderate	Arm rotate/elevates
Cranium (head)	Easy/close	High/none	Minimal	Minimal	Maximum	Percuss; crown/base
Clavicle	Easy/close	Moderate	High	High	Moderate	Percussion
Costae (ribs)	Easy/close	High/low	Minimal	Moderate	Minimal	Percussion; floating
Coxae (hips)	Moderate	Moderate	High	Minimal	Minimal	Body rotation
Gluteus	Situational	Minimal	Moderate	Minimal	Minimal	Leg/all body motion
Sartorius	Moderate	Moderate	High	Moderate	Minimal	Controls knee/hip
Quadriceps	Situational	Moderate	Moderate	Moderate	Minimal	Leg extensors
Hamstrings	Situational	Minimal	High	Minimal	Moderate	Leg/knee flexor
Genu (knee)	Situational	Front high	High	Minimal	Moderate	Ground-fight; kick
Gastro~ (calf)	Situational	Minimal	Moderate	Moderate	Moderate	Ground-fight; kick
Tarsus (foot)	Situational	Moderate	Mid-high	Moderate	Moderate	Ground-fight; kick

PACMAN (WITH TEETH)!

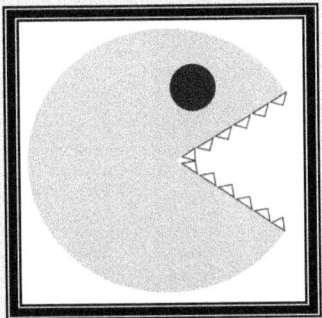

Like special teams in football, there are a few blade techniques that are highly situation-dependent and therefore not often seen or taught. Among these is the half-open/half-closed "snipping" maneuver (colloquially referred to as "the Pac Man move"), which can only be performed with a folder. More particularly, this move really works best with a Bram Frank folder because that tool is specifically designed to be used both open (as a slicing tool) and closed (as an impact tool).

By adopting a specialized grip (best learned directly from a Modular instructor), the practitioner can use the tool in its closed configuration, but lever the blade to a partially open—but not locked—position here-and-there in order to snip or grab flesh or cloth by then snapping the jaws shut!

While the advantages to adding this technique to the toolbox, including the ability to deploy measured force (more than impact/less than lethal), are apparent, it comes with a degree of risk, because this specialized grip—especially if not performed properly, can weaken the practitioner's grasp on the tool. Keeping in mind the first principle—accessibility—this technique should be employed both judiciously and expertly.

♦ JOHN RALSTON ♦

—VIRGINIA—

My second time attending Martial Arts Mania in Jacksonville, Florida, had a huge impact in my martial arts training. This three-day long training camp featuring Grandmaster George Dillman, Professor Wally Jay, and Professor Remy Presas was painful but amazing. I had been studying the art of Ryukyu Kempo under the late Grandmaster Ed Lake for many years. He insisted that I take all opportunities learn from Professors Jay and Presas whenever I possibly could.

I recall being anxious at the start of Professor Presas' first training session. I was working with sticks, and was still feeling somewhat awkward with keeping up with the instruction (the many finger-locks I had practiced during Professor Jay's Small Circle Jujitsu session right before certainly did not help my dexterity). Still, I tried my best to replicate the motions and patterns and understand the techniques being demonstrated. Professor Presas walked around the training floor to assist and provide correction to those who needed it. After some time, he spotted me and greeted me warmly by name. It had been at least a year since I first met him and I was shocked that he remembered me by name. *"John you have been practicing, it is very good! You still live in Florida?"* he said proudly. I replied that I still was residing in Florida. The Professor instructed me to stay where I was as he disappeared into a crowd of people.

He reemerged a short time later followed by a tall, thin man sporting a mullet type of hairstyle, including a very long rat tail braid. I had noticed him earlier, staying towards the back of the room and keeping to himself. It seemed that he might be a kindred-spirit introvert. He seemed to stand out from the oceans of people wearing karate or Arnis uniforms. Rather, he was sporting a sweatshirt with cut-off sleeves and baggy workout pants in a bright blaze of neon, and no belt denoting rank. I remember thinking he was representing 90s fashion! He had racket-ball goggles around his neck, and I noted that his Arnis cane was wrapped with tape at the base like a tennis racket. On his hands were fingerless weightlifting gloves.

The Professor said, *"John, this is Bram. He is moving to Miami and he will teach you!"* He then turned to Bram and said, *"This is John. You will show him the way!"* With that, I became a student of Master-at-Arms, Bram Frank. Bram stayed with me and my training partner that day, helping us try to absorb what Professor Presas taught. He had an insight and intensity that was remarkable and surrounded him almost like an aura. In the many years since that day, Bram and I have laughingly recalled that I was the only student he can never get rid of since Remy Presas gave me to him.

Soon after that camp, I began training regularly with Bram at Glenn Mehlman's dojo in Miami Beach. It was then that I joined the core group of Bram Frank students, along with Jody Barnett-Mehlman, Tony Torre, and a select few others. Those early days of training quickly stretched into a decade, spending day-after-day training with both Bram Frank and Ed Lake. Making the most of having both teachers in South Florida, I took a few opportunities to host seminars featuring, "the dynamic duo."

Bram made it very clear from the outset that I had full permission to interrupt his classes, since I was training closely with him and Ed in Modern Arnis and Ryukyu Kempo as well as Small Circle Jujitsu. This was to show where the arts intersected and which pressure-points to use. I would also demonstrate where the kata *bunkai* would align and where principles of Small Circle Jujitsu fit in.

There have been so many significant events in training with Bram over the years. It was an incredible path of discovery, with truly defining moments and innovations for both Bram and me. His creation of Form Five, including "walking the blocks," identified the blocking movements and footwork of Modern Arnis. This can be paired with its striking counterparts, making it possible to perform it as a two-person drill as well as a solo form. Designed for use in tournaments, Form Six is often presented as a spotlight for Modern Arnis movements and concepts.

A pivotal event for me was transitioning from stick to blade. Bram really took a favorite Professor Presas' phrase—*"It is all the same"*—to heart. If you spend any amount of time training with Bram, you may notice him referencing Wing Chun positions and movements when teaching Modern Arnis (some know that Wing Chun includes edged weapons). It stands to reason, then, that there are several seamless transitions between the two arts. Professor Presas seldom taught blade, and when he did, it was to only a select few. For large groups, the Professor used defense against the knife as context rather than specifically knife fighting. But it is all the same…

From his earliest days, Bram was passionate about the art of the blade, and Professor Presas knew his student. The Professor facilitated this in several ways, including referring Bram to others to gain even more knowledge, so that he would later go on to define the relationship between blade and stick. During this period, Bram attended many training events, including the renowned Riddle of Steel. There, he would meet and share knowledge with other martial arts masters, like Datu Kelly Worden. In recognition of his progress in blade-centric Modern Arnis, Professor Presas bequeathed two of the Presas family *bolos* to Bram [one belonged to his grandfather and the other to an uncle]. It was clear to the Professor that Bram's dedication to his art and his passion and respect should be recognized.

For Bram, the blade is much more than just an edged tool. An artist at heart, Bram would become a designer of knives that were both practical as well as elegant. The Professor's eyes lit up when Bram showed him the first designs and early prototypes. I believe that training with Bram during this pivotal time, as he transitioned from the more well-known traditional stick guy into expressing Modern Arnis as a blade art, was a transformative experience for me as well. Bram's growth, both as a martial artist and blade designer, has given me a unique perspective into this representation of Modern Arnis. Common Sense Self Defense/Street Combat (CSSD/CS), or what the core members affectionately call "Bram Arnis" is practiced world-wide and pays tribute to the Professor's passion to share his beloved art.

—John Ralston

IX. BODY SHIFTING [λ]
Target, Range, Angle & Elevation

PRINCIPLE: BODY SHIFT TO CONTROL RANGE AND ANGLE

BODY SIFTING!

To this day, instructors who trained with Remy Presas find themselves unable to avoid lovingly mimicking his accent when giving the commands he once issued to them. Among these is "body sifting" (*sans* "h," so much so that the written sub-titles to an early video of the Professor's actually use this spelling)! However it is pronounced, the fact remains that when the Professor saw anyone executing strikes from a fixed stance, he immediately recognized that they were new to his art and had much to learn about 'the Flow.'

Targeting: Some knife-fighting schools teach disemboweling, artery-severing, and vital point cutting or stabbing, but almost all of these decidedly lethal targets are within what might be described as 'the vertical core' of the opponent's torso. As a result, in order to be able to reach these core targets, the practitioner must get close enough that he himself is also in range.

GRAY'S ARC RANGE FOR TARGETS IN THE VERTICAL CORE

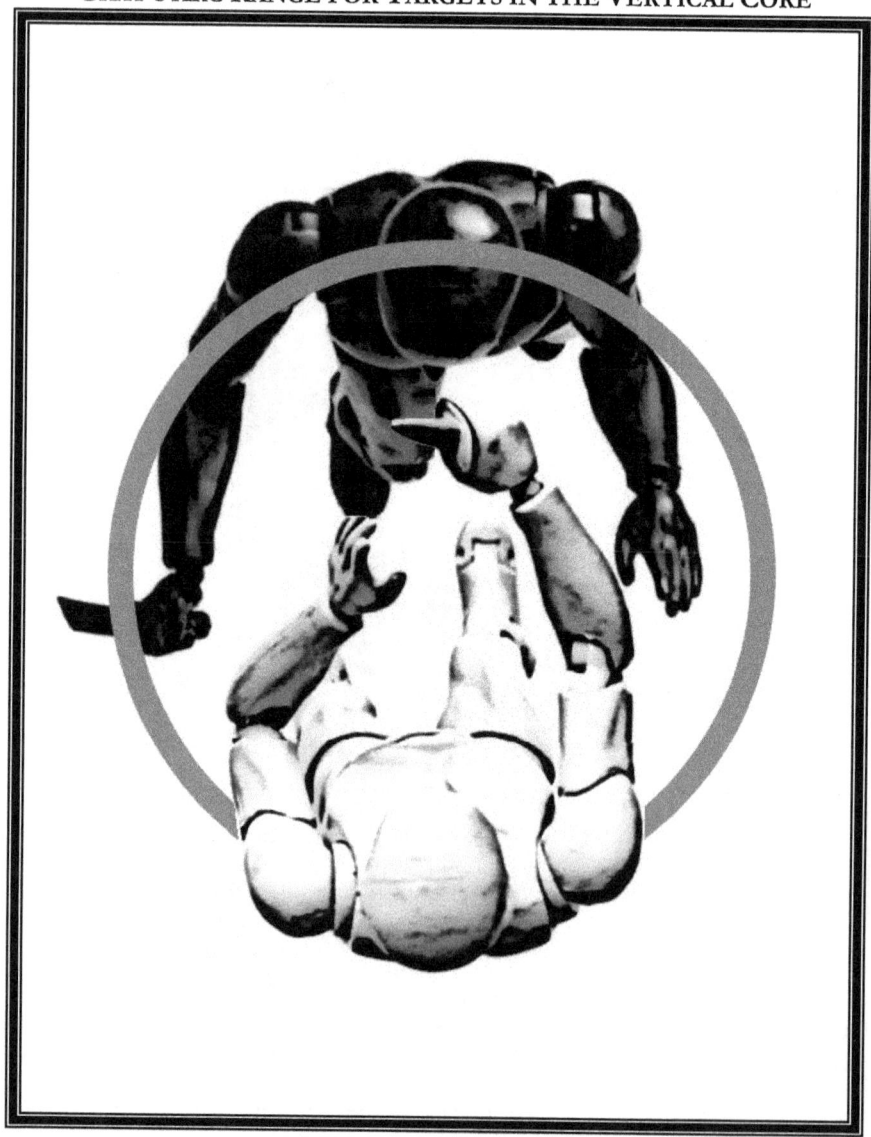

BLACK'S ARC RANGE FOR TARGETS AT THE EXTREMITIES

Bram's approach, by contrast, focuses on disabling the attacker's arm—what Remy Presas and other Filipino masters call, *"de-fanging the snake."* And while the ethical and legal merits of this approach are discussed elsewhere in this work, the *tactical* advantage it provides is one of the most compelling bases for studying this art. If your opponent must reach for your core, and you only need to reach for his attacking limb, the playing field tilts heavily in your favor. And while your wrist might still technically be in range for the opponent, this is likely not the target that he was originally aiming for.

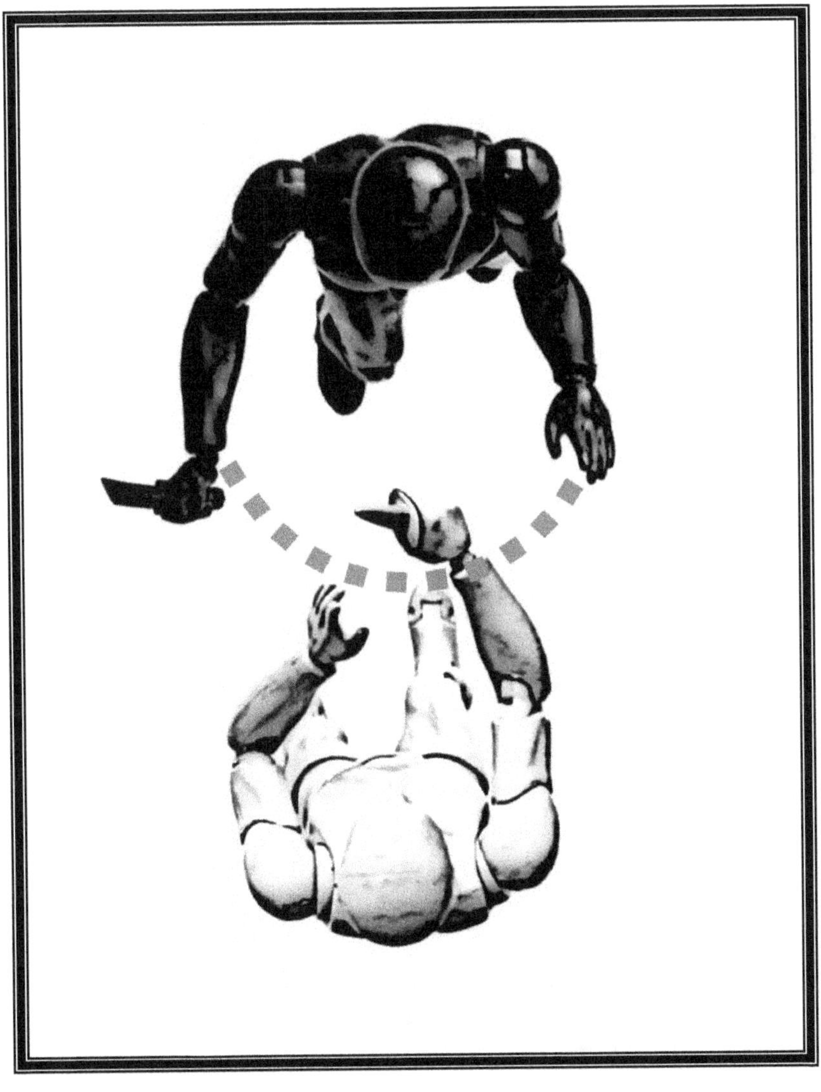

OVERLAPPING ARC RANGES FOR TARGETS (CORE/EXTREMITIES)

Keep in mind that Gray is reaching for core targets (which are out of his range) while Black needs only to reach the wrist (which is within his range).

Angle/Displacement: In addition, as Bram teaches, when the practitioner is defending, he is already a half a beat behind because he must react to the attacker's first move. This gives rise to a few imperatives, the first of which is body displacement. The best block, as they say, is: *"Don't be there!"* Accordingly, the first thing the practitioner typically does—even before intercepting/attempting to intercept the strike—is to displace the target (head, shoulder, stomach) by stepping/shifting out of harm's way, while ideally keeping his/her own target in range. This way the check and counter-attack can be launched from a position of relative safety.

GRAY'S ANGLE OF ENGAGEMENT

Now, even though Gray and Black remain equidistant from one another, because of the different angular orientations when Black steps off line, the field in which Gray can engage Black differs markedly from the field in which Black can engage Gray (and remember: Gray is aiming for the core).

BLACK'S ANGLE OF ENGAGEMENT

With one simple sidestep, Black simultaneously withdraws the targets Gray would like to reach from Gray's field of engagement and at the same time remains within range of—or even closer to—the targets he would like to engage (wrist, forearm, etc.).

OVERLAPPING ANGLES OF ENGAGEMENT

When displayed in an overlapping fashion, it is clear that Black needs to reach less far, in a forward orientation, to strike his target(s), while Gray needs to reach much farther, toward his offside, and still won't be able to reach any of the core targets.

Elevation: Finally, Bram teaches his students to think in three tactical dimensions (in other words, don't forget the z-axis). Accordingly, as illustrated in the preceding overhead shots, when intercepting a #1 strike, while the opponent is technically within range of the practitioner's wrist in the horizontal plane (even though this is likely not his intended target), he is cutting on a *higher* line than the practitioner's countering interception.

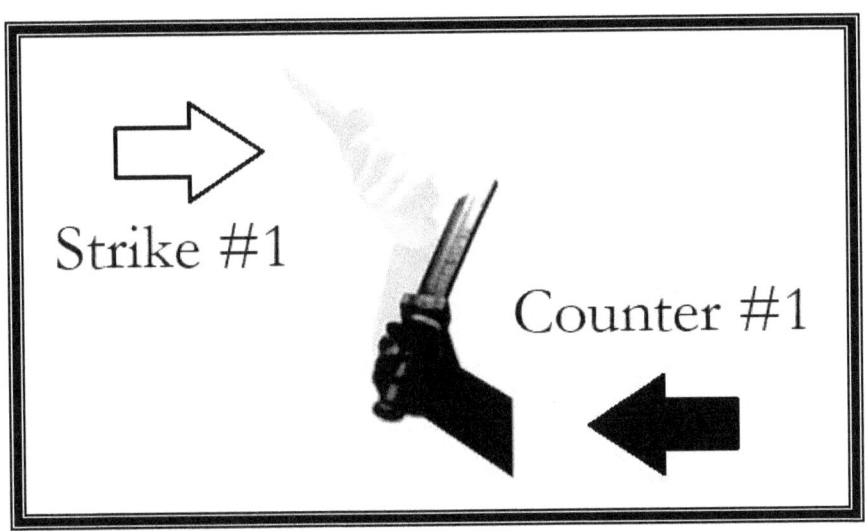

SHIFTING PERSPECTIVES

I had what might be described as a pretty savage upbringing—it was hard, but we also learned to defend ourselves at an early age. I was around eight years old when I was first introduced to the art of fencing, and from that point on, I was pretty much a martial arts junkie...

Over the decades that followed, I trained in a wide variety of arts, including traditional *karate*, *kajukenbo*, and *kali*. This sometimes required working early morning shifts so that I could commute for several hours to and from the *dojo* in the evening (so I don't have a whole lot of sympathy for people who complain about having to drive across town to attend class)!

After earning senior ranks in several arts, I eventually opened a small *dojo* of my own, teaching a group of hand-picked students out of my modified garage. Because of both our size and our standards, we are a very selective school, with applicants being pre-screened by one of my senior instructors and even then, sometimes being wait-listed for a year or more.

By the time I met Bram, I had been training for decades, so it's fair to say I was no stranger to the arts, including bladed weapons. In 2006 or 2007, a friend of mine who ran a local school had Bram in for a seminar and invited me to come along.

I think Bram and I recognized each other as kindred spirits right away. I was immediately intrigued by the way he was able to distill and convey complex concepts while remaining so approachable (despite his seniority), and, as anyone who knows him will attest, his passion is contagious. For his part, it didn't take long for Bram to come up to me and say, *"I notice you were nodding in all the right places..."*

The next step in our relationship involved inviting Bram to come teach at my home school. In some ways, the bonding process began from the moment he first arrived at my home and broke bread with me and my family. For old-school guys like Bram (and me), this kind of thing really matters—it's important to observe these traditional social conventions.

Once on the mat, I recall that he began by asking how I felt about starting out with the long blade (*bolo*) before moving on to the kind of material which will likely be more familiar to those reading this work. From that day on, we became part of the same warrior tribe.

ORION, THE HUNTER, ARMED WITH BLADE

Over the years that followed, I was fortunate to attend many more seminars with Bram, including some with the kind of people in attendance who had to be treated as *"not really there…"* One of the most powerful concepts that Bram manages to convey in his teaching is the importance of distance and timing—not as two separate concepts, but in combination—through body shifting. Mastering this unitary concept dramatically changes the balance of power in any engagement, and in helping me to find and follow this thread, Bram shaved at least a decade off my own journey. In an era when people can at least try to learn almost anything online, many fail to appreciate the true value of learning at the hands of a real master, and Bram is such a teacher.

—Eric Filippenko

X. GIVE & TAKE
The Cornerstone

Common to almost every bladed art system, and dating back to the Bronze Age, is some form of upward 'warding-off' movement, reminiscent of an open umbrella or snow slipping off an angled roof tile. This kind of ward is often featured as a component in "give-and-take drills" in which two training partners work together to exchange a series of attacks and defenses, often reversing roles after the first completion of the pattern.

These give-and-take drills are the cornerstones of Bram's system, beginning with the so-called "1-4-12" pattern. It is first taught in standard (right-hand-against-right-hand) with equal forward grips, but can be performed in any of the other possible combinations (reverse 1-4-12, backward 1-4-12, opposite side 2-3-12, etc...). And students have absorbed this first drill, they can then move on to others:

1. **1-4-12:** The foundational building block;
2. **2-3-12:** Mirror of the 1-4-12 attacks/defenses;
3. **1-2-2:** Transitions from high-line to low-line and vice-versa;
4. **5-2-4:** Introduces the thrust.

OPEN POSITION [1-4-12]

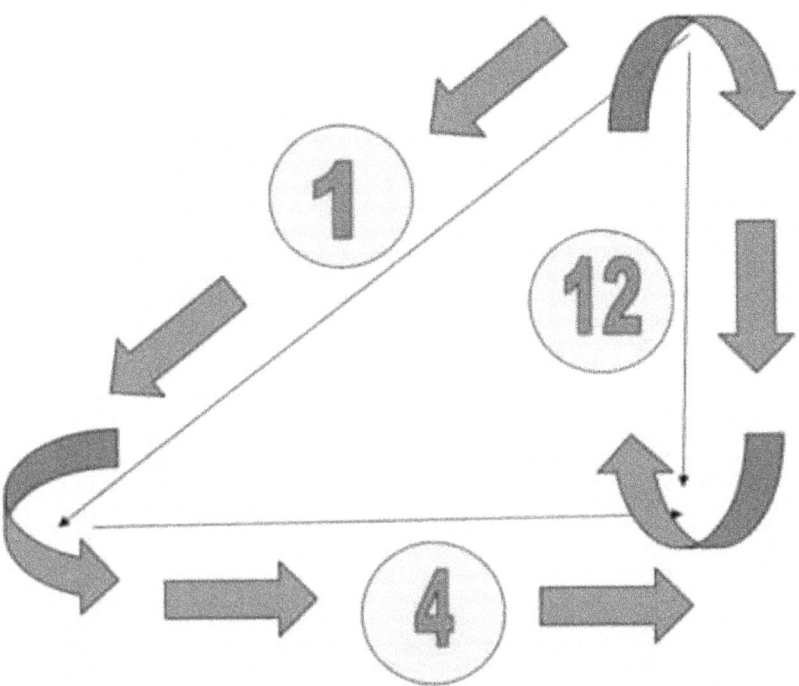

STRIKE #1 & RESPONSE

STRIKE #4 & RESPONSE

STRIKE #12 & RESPONSE

As Bram says, you can't (and shouldn't) learn martial arts from a book. In many ways, a two-dimensional snapshot is a lousy way to present three-dimensional movements. Even with video, something is lost in translation. As a result, the best way to make progress on your martial journey is by finding a flesh-and-blood instructor at a brick-and-mortar location, however...

CLOSED POSITION [2-3-12]

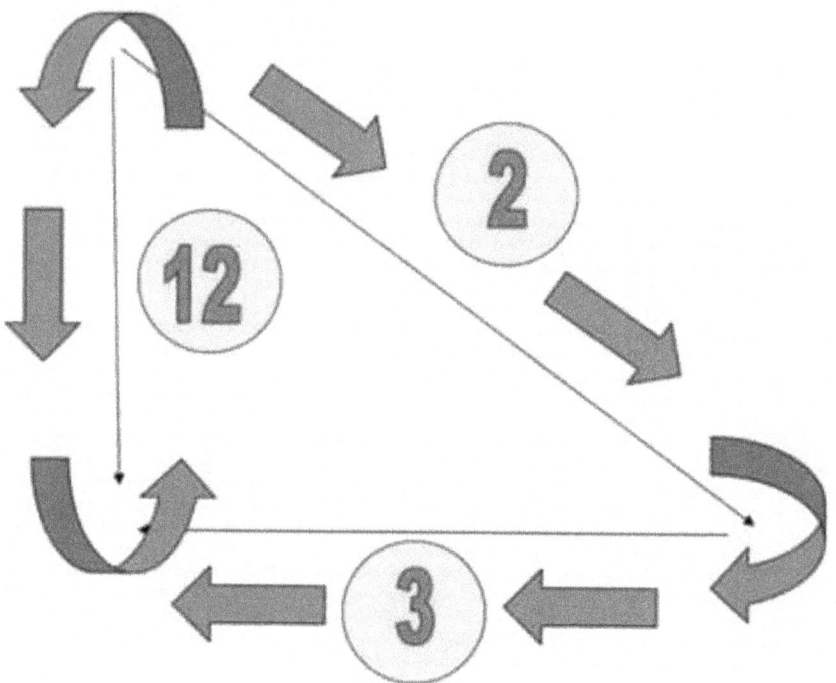

STRIKE #2 & RESPONSE   STRIKE #3 & RESPONSE   STRIKE #12 & RESPONSE

> ... having acknowledged the limitations of paper presentations, books do still serve an important role in the process: They can be the catalyst to begin down a particular path (as with Bram); they can serve as a guide by providing you with the accounts of other travelers—both ancient and modern; and at least this one provides a template with which to chronicle your own journey.

HIGH LINE [1-2-2]

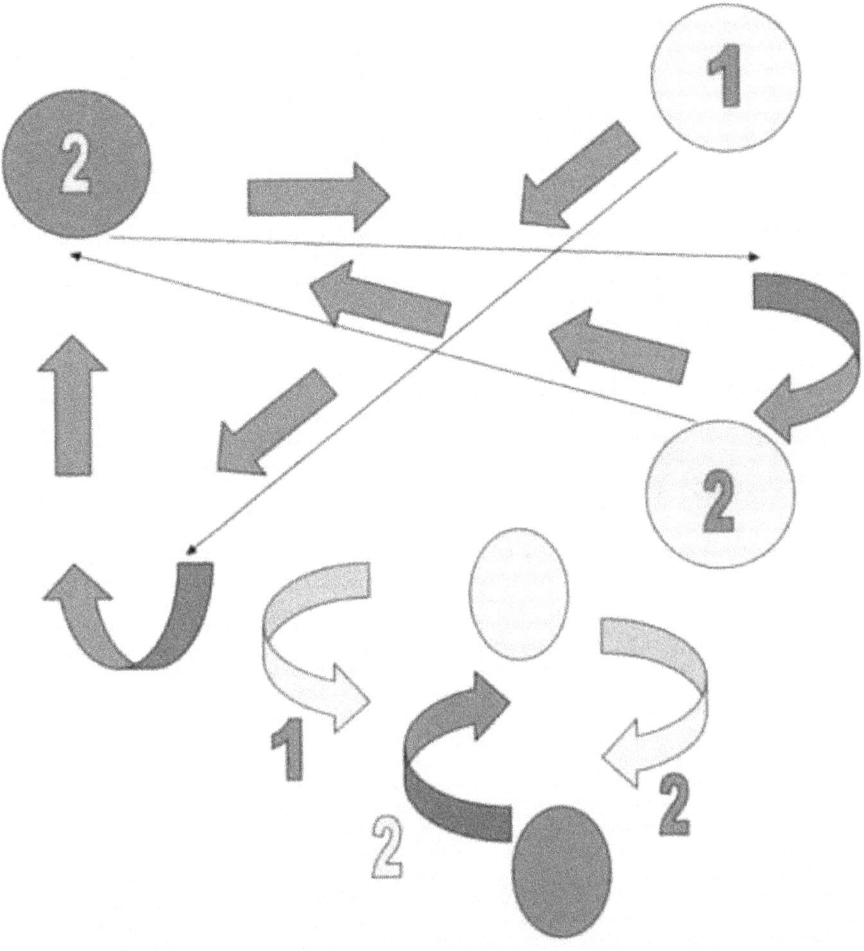

STRIKE #1 & RESPONSE

STRIKE #2(O) & RESPONSE

STRIKE #2(C) & RESPONSE

THE FIRST THREE SETS FROM THE STRIKER'S PERSPECTIVE

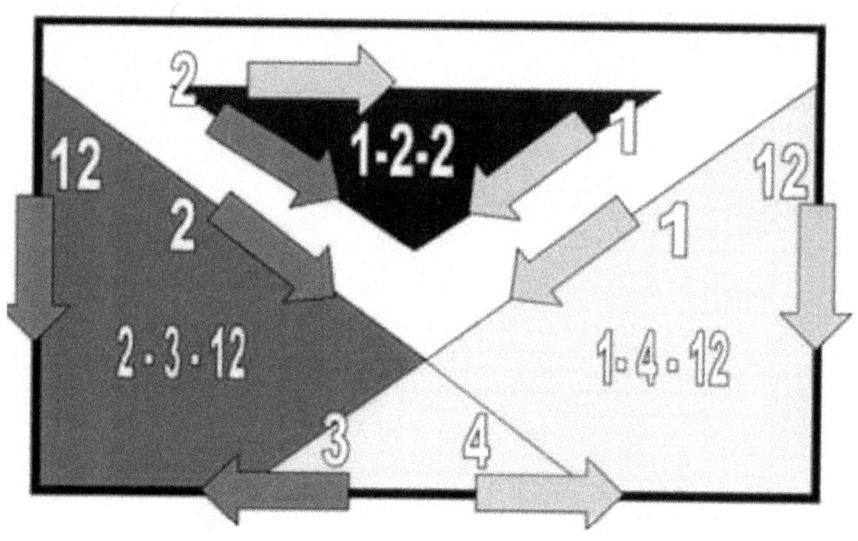

THE FIRST THREE SETS FROM THE DEFENDER'S PERSPECTIVE

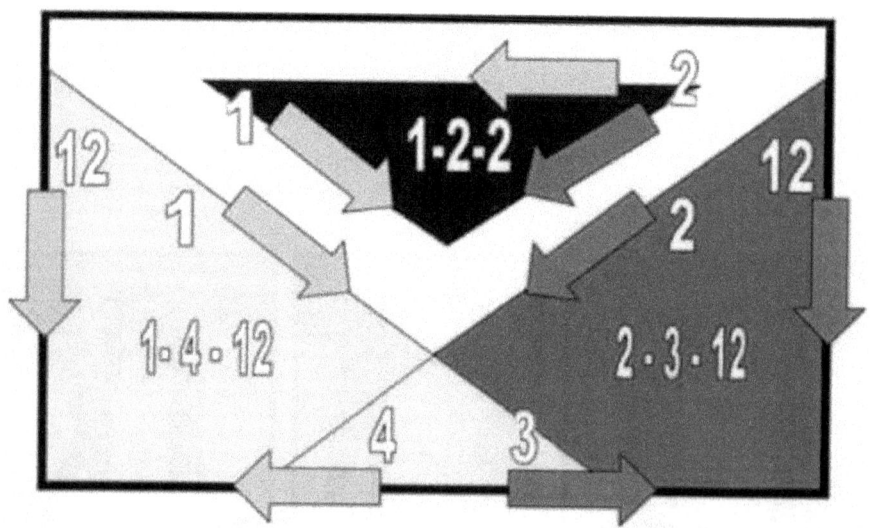

Body Shifting II: The secret here is that the knife already 'knows' how to cut, and the practitioner's job is simply to stay out of the way, allowing the tool to do its job, whether it is being held in the left hand or the right, tip up or tip down, by the attacker or by the defender. In most cases, the knife's position remains the same; it is the practitioner's body which shifts to accommodate deployment of the tool.

Spacing and Structure: Just as the *body* moves to accommodate the way the *tool* works, so the *technique* must be performed in a way that accommodates the way the human *body* works. For example, when forestalling an overhead #12 attack, the practitioner must move in close to the attacker (as well as out of the line of fire) in order make a strong umbrella block. The structure of the human body dictates this spacing.

ATTACK: GRAY STRIKES #1, BLACK INTERCEPTS WRIST WITH HIS BLADE

COUNTER: BLACK SLICES THE WRIST AND COUNTER-CUTS #4

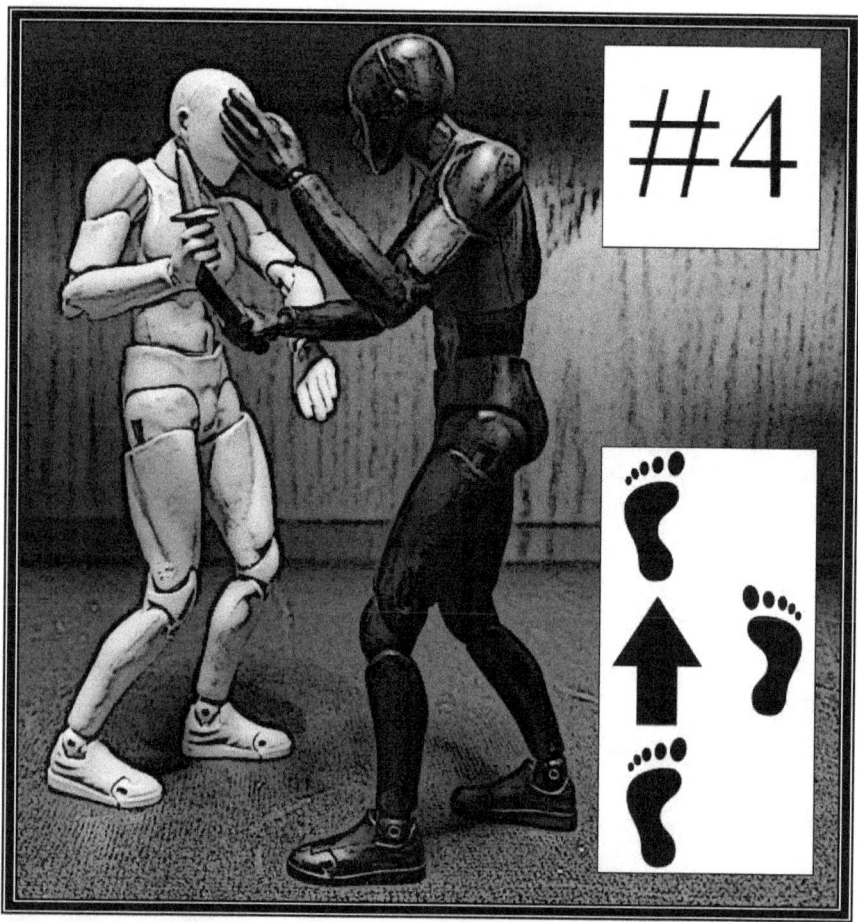

ATTACK: GRAY STRIKES #12, BLACK LIFTS HIS BLADE TO INTERCEPT [μ]

#12

COUNTER: BLACK STEPS 'THROUGH,' CUTS WRIST, COUNTERS #1…

♦ JOHN RALSTON ♦
—VIRGINIA—
SUMBRADA AND *CROSSADA*

Bram uses the *sumbrada* drill (in conjunction with the perspectives) to disassemble and reassemble Modern Arnis. The principles and the grips introduce additional elements, including stirring, decision points, and switch points. Moving into other drills and motions, they weave the tapestry of Modern Arnis and combat. *Sumbrada* uses three angles: #1, #4, and #12, and starts with standard-forward-equal perspective.

This drill involves two people switching the role of attacker and defender. As you advance, the attacker might use the same follow up motion to maintain his role as attacker, forcing the defender to flow and counter, leading to a new set of circumstances. There are many variations to *sumbrada*, such as 2-3-12 and 5-2-4.

You can add to or subtract elements from these drills after a basic flow is establish, and errors in positioning and movement can be addressed and rectified. You can change the perspective of both or just one participant. You can employ a standard perspective versus a backwards or mirror perspective. You should go slowly at first so as to reduce confusion. Indicate your intention and allow yourself and your partner to discover the connections. You might also introduce reverse grip and the variations that can occur between equal and unequal options. You can introduce dual blades, returning to standard-forward-equal, but with a tool in each hand. Then you can progress through the perspectives and grip variations before again resuming standard-forward-equal.

It is important always to start and finish each modular segment in standard-forward-equal, because you want to build pathways of recognition between what you know best and new material/perspectives. Dual wielding can be an excellent approach for this purpose as you are exploring a new perspective in one hand while revisiting a familiar one in the other hand. For instance, with an edged tool in both hands, using forward grip, your right hand is in standard-forward-equal while your left hand is in backwards-backwards. You can even introduce disarming and counter disarming from the standard-forward-equal perspective instead of grip changes, as well as dual wielding, or perspective shifts, or passing, or stirring. This all builds to the point where you can introduce random decision or switch points in order to introduce new modules.

The FMA concept of *crossada* is basically a scissoring action, crossing and uncrossing the arms with the goal of catching or striking two points of contact (e.g., ventral and dorsal, or anterior and posterior) on the attacking limb. The drill has a specific range for use as well, namely *largo mano*, or long range, defined as: The range at which the attacker can reach your limbs, and vice versa, but neither of you can make contact with the other's torso without closing the gap.

Looking back, I think this was one of the patterns that eventually evolved into Bram's Modular Arnis system. *Crossada* can be employed in a six-count drill using angles #1 through #5 and #12, with one partner serving as attacker, and the other defending, before switching roles. When using an impact tool, such as a stick, it may seem a bit awkward, striking stick-to-stick and scissoring back and forth, but you will absorb many vital principles from working the drill this way, such as body shifting, hip rotation, proper placement, and usage of the check hand, as well as learning to move from the positions you are in, rather than setting up a position before counter attacking or attacking.

When I first started training with Bram, Modern Arnis was primarily an impact tool art, taught with empty hand translation (this is how I and others initially performed the drill). In many schools, it is still taught this way. Under Bram's guidance, however, we quickly modified it, leveraging real-world scenarios and innovating Modern Arnis. Rather than striking stick-to-stick, we began striking stick (or training tool) to limb, but with great restraint to ensure no injuries.

Striking the limb made the drill feel far less awkward and much more sensible, especially when holding an impact tool in each hand. However, when we used only a single impact tool, the passing movement with the live hand seemed to have no real value. We then replaced the impact tool with an edged tool, and the missing pieces fell into place. With the impact tool, using the passing hand to pull the limb across the tool served no real purpose, but with the edged tool, this movement maintains edge-to-limb contact, leading to a deeper cut (combining sticking control and sensitivity with bio-mechanical cutting). The position and function of the live hand became vital, both in terms of better utilization of the edge and in making sure that the live hand did not obstruct our own blade, as well as teaching students to lead with the edge of the tool and not employ the live hand prematurely.

—John Ralston

THE SHADOW WARRIOR

Please allow me to introduce someone: ***The shadow warrior.***

Perhaps the best training partner you will ever have, this man (or woman) with no name is never too busy or too tired to train with you. He/she always knows what you want to work on, and typically improves in lock step with your own performance. This is because he/she is a figment of your own imagination.

If this idea has never occurred to you before, don't be too hasty in dismissing it. This is much more than an imaginary friend (or enemy). Study after scientific study confirms the power of visualization in improving athletic performance across a wide variety of disciplines. For training in the combat arts, it is *essential* that the fighter be able to conjure up a mental sparring partner at will (think shadow-boxing). And the amount of mental energy it takes to construct and operate this wraith—not just think about it, but truly see (and sometimes even feel) its movements—rivals some of the most demanding physical workouts.

Another thing that recommends the adoption and perfection of this mode of practice is that, like Bram's 'thumb-knife,' you will never be without this essential training tool. Even when training solo. Even during a lockdown. Even when physically laid up. And one more thing: Bram calls his imaginary training partner, "Figment the Dragon" and even says that Figment sometimes wins…

XI. PATTERNS OF FORCE
Don't Miss the Woods for the Trees

This is a keypad. Imagine if I told you that your passcode to open the door which it protects was: 1-4-7-8-9-6-3-2, but you could not write it down—you just had to memorize it. Granted, perhaps not the most daunting task imaginable, but it is one digit longer than the human brain's typical telephone-number-length comfort level, and, as anyone who has ever locked themselves out because of multiple failed passcode attempts can attest, it is not the easiest thing to remember either, especially under pressure.

Now imagine that instead of trying to memorize this eight number sequence in the abstract, all you had to do was remember the visual pattern: Beginning in the top left corner, simply 'walk the perimeter' counterclockwise.

The Art of The Blade

Much easier, right? In fact, it is because of the very ease with which these patterns can be recognized that cutting edge digital keypad locks now randomly reposition the numbers each time a code needs to be entered. And while this may thwart the use of this system when it comes to keypads, the principle remains valid: It is easier to learn, remember, and reproduce patterns than a series of individual components.

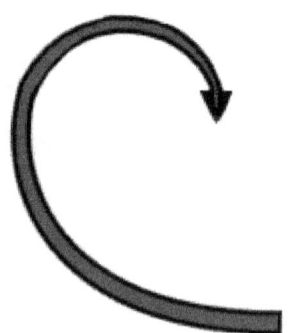

Horizontal-to-Vertical: One of the core patterns of Modular—especially when using the CRMIPT—is 'horizontal-to-vertical.' For example, when defending against jab or thrust to the head or face, the practitioner can intercept with a right hand open-to-closed motion on the horizontal plane and then respond with a vertical counterstrike. This pattern—which involves not only right-to-left and down-to-up, but also rear-to-forward and up-to-down—is seen again and again in Modular, and forms an important part of the foundation of the art.

| PRINCIPLE: DON'T MEMORIZE, LEARN PATTERNS |

Finite Options: Patterns are important not only in defense, but also in anticipating the offense. Part of the challenge of defending oneself is having no idea of where the next attack is coming from. In an effort to impose some order on this chaos, the Modular system takes advantage of the fact that there are only two ways to hold a knife (forward and reverse grip) and two hands (left and right) in which to hold it, giving rise to a maximum of sixteen possible configurations in any engagement involving two combatants.

| PRINCIPLE: PREPARE FOR FINITE OPTIONS |

Patterns of Force: High Line, Low Line (Diagonal, Vertical): Another helpful aspect of 'Bram-speak' is the use of the terms: "high line," "low line," "diagonal," and "vertical," so that rather than getting caught up in the minutiae of which hand is cutting or deflecting on which side, the practitioner can envisage general zones of engagement. In this way, a high line strike can be *either* a #1 or a #2; a low line strike can be either a #3 or #4; and so on (and keep in mind that module 1-2-2 is the tool for transitioning from the high line to the low line and back).

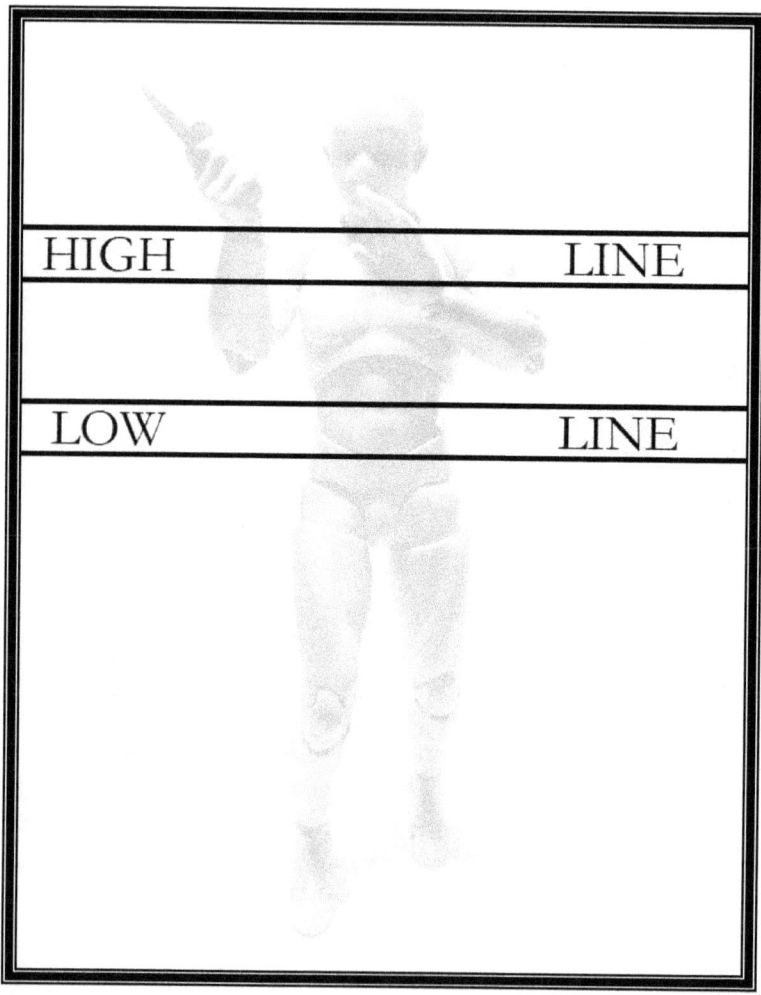

Training Tip: When identifying similar patterns (such as intercepting a #5 and a #12), Bram will often assist students in grasping the larger, abstract picture by asking them: *"Where are you in space and time?"*

With these three lines in mind, it can now be seen that the attacks in the foundational 1-4-12 give-and-take drill cut on or toward the low line; the 2-3-12 drill mirrors these attacks on the opposite side; the 1-2-2 drill teach practitioners to transition *between* high and low line; and 5-2-4 adds a thrust into the mix.

> **MULTIMEDIA CODE †**
>
> If you accept the proposition that a picture is worth a thousand words, then a thirty second video clip is worth about a million (modern video runs at about thirty frames per second).
>
> As we have reached the halfway point in this book, we have run out of free clips on Bram's pivotshare site, but you have now earned a three month all access pass using the code: **ARTOFTHEBLADE**. Using this code to access video of the material that follows will assist in your training immeasurably.

FINITE NUMBERS

In keeping with this process of simplification, at the end of the day, there are only five basic strikes to consider with a few areas of defensive variation and overlap, making for a total of twelve patterns:

#1: Two variations:
(i) Slice (draw) down to low line, counter #4;
(ii) Guide past/over to high line, counter #2;

#2: Four variations:
(i) Hand check, high line cut, counter #2;
(ii) Trapped blade, nut-and-bolt, counter #1;
(iii) Biceps slice to low line, counter #4;
(iv) Blade check, low line cut, counter #3;

#3: One approach: Drop the open hand forearm for bone-to-bone block, knife draw slice, counter #12;

#4: Two approaches:
(i) Drop the open hand forearm for bone-to-bone block, knife draw slice, counter #12;
(ii) Same set up, counter #5 instead of #12.

#5: One approach: Drop tip ward, slice up, counter #2;

#12: Two variations:
(i) Open umbrella, counter #1;
(ii) Closed umbrella (slant), counter #2.

It Is All The Same: Continuing with the goal of avoiding getting bogged down in idiosyncratic details, Bram encourages a focus on *concepts*—for example, forehand and backhand—rather than rigid rules—for instance: "Left hand strikes from right-to-left at a 45-degree angle...".

In this way, low, middle, or high cuts or thrusts to the opponent's vertical axis all fall into the category of midline attacks, and Bram is not too fussy about which one the student chooses to employ on any given occasion. Footwork is similarly flexible, calling for steps and shifts as needed to optimize the range-to-target. Common the virtually all defenses, however, are four fundamental components:

> **A: Avoid** getting cut (stepping, body shifting);
>
> **B: Blade** checks/cuts (in rare instances, live hand checks first);
>
> **C: Check** with live hand (cut sometimes *follows* a live hand check);
>
> **D: Decide** what your counter will be...

For learning purposed, these components may be ordered slightly differently depending on the technique (#1=ABCD; #4=CABD; #12=BCAD); when performed, they should flow together seamlessly (and often simultaneously rather than mechanically "on the beat").

ABANIKO DOUBLE ACTION

Here is a code within a code: The elegant arcs that comprise the CSSD-SC/MBC² symbol are actually a visual representation of the Modern Arnis technique: *abaniko* double action. Why this particular technique? As anyone who trained with Professor Presas can tell you: Because it was his favorite...

♦ CHAD BAILEY ♦

—FLORIDA—

Bram is first and foremost, my friend and big brother.

We share so many of the same memories and stories of our teacher, Remy Presas. During his classes, Bram will often say, *"When he moves, he is cut!"* and it brings back the memory of Remy saying that many times with a stick in his hand, and the majority of the students scratching their heads while only some of us knew what he was getting at…

Other sayings, like: *"Go with the Flow," "It is all the same," "Make it your own," "The art within your art,"* and *"You have it, it is already yours,"* all inspire memories of our master. I see so much of Remy in Bram when he moves and teaches.

Bram is also my teacher. He has so much to share and he teaches the reality of the blade—it's Modern Arnis with edged weapons. My training with Bram has included: Conceptual Modern Arnis, Modular Knife, *bolo*, *desangut*, and CRMIPT, as well as Modern Arnis cane and *bolo Anyos*. My favorite training with Bram is Presas bolo, which is known as, "the Soul of Arnis."

Bram is an uncle to my sons and has a bond with both which is separate from my interaction with him. My older son, Zayon (now twenty-one), has trained with Bram since he was eight years old. Jared, the typical teenager, does not want to train very often, but he is always up front at Bram's classes at our camps.

In the late 80s and early 90s, Bram and I attended many seminars together, including those in the Philadelphia area hosted by Michael Bates. Other senior practitioners like Ray Goss and Chas Terry were always in attendance. Bram and I also attended the annual Summer Camps in Massachusetts at Mount Holyoke College, hosted by Richard Roy. These were brutal four-day camps from Thursday to Sunday, and mostly ran from nine am to nine pm! Lee Lowry, Brian Zawilinski, Tom Bolden, Doug Pierre and another of my teachers, Billy Bryant, were all regulars there. The summer camp of 1991 is where I received my black belt from Remy. Bram and I also attended the "Triple Threat" seminars in Delaware hosted Jim and Judy Clapp because it was impossible to pass up the opportunity to train with Remy, Wally Jay and George Dillman (and there was always infectious laughter when they were all together).

In 1995, I moved from Santa Fe, New Mexico, where I had attended graduate school, to Miami Beach, Florida. Even with a Doctor of Oriental Medicine, I needed to pay the rent so I found restaurant work on Miami Beach as a bus boy. I was quickly moved to host because I could easily talk to people. During this time, I would get out of work at four pm and go to the beach to train for a few hours. A few of the other waiters, bus boys and cooks started to join me and soon I had a five-to-six person class running twice a week.

A few weeks later, one of Bram's students went to his class and told him there was a guy teaching sticks on the beach. Bram's response was: *"Who is this guy teaching Arnis on the beach? My beach!?"* He sent a student by my class to check me out. The student was polite and respectful, and we trained together. When he reported back to Bram, his reactions was: *"Oh... It's Chad baby!"* (Remy's nickname for me, which Bruce Chiu often recalls him shouting at the top of his lungs each time he would see me at the camp in Orlando).

Bram became a regular guest instructor at my classes, and my students, at his seminars. Moving back to the East Coast allowed me to re-connect with my Modern Arnis family, particularly in Florida. Bram and I attended all the camps Bruce Chiu hosted—so many fantastic camps with many regulars like Ray Dionaldo and Fred Lazo. Many of my Progressive Arnis students attended with me, tested, and earned rank in Modern Arnis this way.

After Remy's passing in 2001, I began to attend many of Bram's seminars at the Hialeah Police Department, the Hollywood dojo, and throughout Florida (this is also when I added Modular Knife concepts to the Progressive Arnis curriculum).

In 2010, I became Bram's acupuncturist, using regular treatments to improve his health and wellness. We must keep him healthy and happy! In 2012, at Bram's urging, I accepted a Founder's award from the World Head of Family Sokeship Council and the title: Grandmaster of Progressive Arnis. This was not something I had considered or even wanted, but Bram made me realize that my curriculum and teaching should be acknowledged. Bram said, *"You did what Remy told us to do: Make it your own!"* Thank you for your confidence in me, my brother.

My students, family, and I have traveled across the country to train with Bram. The most fun are his birthday bashes in Vancouver, Washington, at Mish Handwerker's school. My whole family and a couple of my black belts will be attending the birthday *Bolo* Instructor Camp in 2021! I have made many new friends through Bram: Roger Agbulos, Mish Handwerker, Tony Torre, Vince Oller, Pedro Rodriguez and many more. These connections are priceless to me and I reference them almost daily (even though Bram might not know it).

I own many of Bram's blades, from folders to fixed blades, and from *bolos* to *desanguts*. My wife carries a MySo and has a CRMIPT in her car for emergencies. Both of my sons have been taught to handle and use knives and are particularly fond of Bram's live blades and drones.

It recently came to my attention that the majority of my students have at least one of Bram's tools, and most of my black belts use one of his blades as their EDC. More often than not these days, Bram and I end up teaching at the same events, be it one of my camps, where he is a guest instructor, or a conference or gathering where we are both guest instructors. Either way, I am honored to share the stage with my big brother. And we both know Remy is smiling down on us, seeing two of his students teaching together.

I love you Brother Bram.

—Chad Bailey

XII. SWITCH AND DECISIONS POINTS
Go With the Flow

Agos. Ryu. Shùn. Retzev. The Flow. Whether you express this concept in Tagalog, Japanese, Chinese, Hebrew, or English, the theme remains the same: The best way to deal with a situation or an obstacle is to adapt to it. Woodworkers will tell you that modern power tools can hack and chop their way cleanly through even the toughest lumber, but respecting the natural grains and patterns of this living material is the way to produce a masterpiece. And every surfer knows that you have no choice but to work with the great ocean currents; never against them.

After **nine** decades in the arts, *Wei Kuen Do* Founder and Headmaster Leo Fong puts it this way: *"You don't steer life; you surf it!"*

✣ *Agos* (Tagalog): Anyone who spent a single hour with Remy Presas on the mat will have heard him talk about "the Flow." It is the *sine qua non* of Modern Arnis. When he used this term, most commonly, he was referring to the practitioner's ability to move effortlessly from one technique to another; from defense to offense; and from form to form.

✣ *Ryu* (Japanese): This term for a martial tradition—as in: the *Komaru Ryu*—evolved from pictograms showing knowledge being carried on a river. In this way, 'the Flow' can be seen as a mighty tributary along which age-old wisdom is carried into the modern era.

✣ *Shùn* (Chinese): The seven flows described in ancient treatises on Chinese martial practice refer to the way in which power should be smoothly transmitted from shoulders to elbows to hands to fingers; from waist to hips to knees to feet; and from head to body.

✣ *Retzev* (Hebrew): In *Krav Maga* parlance, *retzev* means "continuous motion," and is a core concept which drives the practitioner to harness the natural power of movement throughout the execution of both defensive and offensive techniques.

All of these ideas echo in a common chamber. They recognize that there is a Force far greater than our own in this world, to be understood and respected. Whether it is the power of natural movement; the strength of tradition; or the effectiveness of instinctive reaction; we only truly reach our potential when we go *with* the flow.

Having established the importance of 'going with the flow,' then, there will inevitably come a point in any engagement when the practitioner encounters an obstacle. Rather than simply exerting more force and pushing forward blindly, Bram teaches students to open their eyes; to flow with *the situation*; and to recognize it as an opportunity to switch things up!

Switch Points: These are moments in an engagement when the practitioner encounters a barrier—usually one created by the opponent—and must find another way forward, commonly by transitioning to another of the basic modules. Because there are elements which are common to each of these modules, the practitioner can use them to shift from one to another seamlessly. A two strike, for example, allows the practitioner to transition between any of the three modules in which this move features, but in order to transition to 1-4-12, it is necessary to choose a different common element because there is no #2 strike in this module.

[†This would be a good place/time to access Bram's video on pivotshare.]

SWITCH POINTS

Lo/Hi Switch: Barrier #4
                     Wedge in/up;
                     Check (hand);
                     Counter #2.

Hi/Lo Switch: Barrier #2
                     Hilt pass;
                     Triceps check;
                     Counter #4.

Decision points: Similar in many ways to switch points, decision points are also opportunities to change things up, but the difference is that they are proactively chosen by the practitioner rather than being reactively deployed in response to an obstacle. They are commonly named for the particular attack which generates the opportunity to choose from multiple defensive options (example: "decision closed 2").

DECISION POINTS

#1: Low line or high line?

#2: [Open] Counter #2 or #4?

#2: [Closed] Counter #1 or #3?

#12: Open or closed umbrella?

The reason that the fourth step in the general defense formula set forth in the previous chapter is *decide* rather than simply *counter* is because the choice of counter *determines* which of the four basic modules the practitioner wishes to work within for the time being.

THE FOUR BASIC MODULES

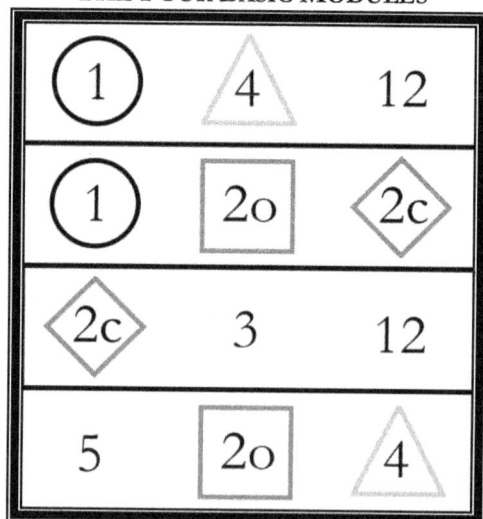

This design by Mish Handwerker illustrates the common threads among the modules, especially 1-2-2, which is the universal coonnecting thread.

HEROES

In navigating life's decision points, we look to our heroes to set the example. A hundred years before Disney popularized the name "John Carter" on the silver screen, *Tarzan* author Edgar Rice Burroughs also dreamed up this space-faring adventurer in his *Barsoom* series of science-fiction novels:

Isaac Asimov and Wolf Wenton turned me onto these books back in the mid-Sixties, and they have been part of me since. I re-read the series every year, and they have taught me so much, including:

† Live by the attributes of friendship, loyalty, and honor, which are core building blocks of character, whether or not others follow or reciprocate.

† You can change the way you look or present yourself, but the inner self doesn't change. We are immutable internally.

† Our beliefs direct our actions.

† It is vital to stick to your beliefs even under pressure—<u>especially</u> under pressure.

† You must love unwaveringly and be willing to do anything to keep and protect that love.

† Never give up, never surrender!

—Bram Frank

♦ JOHN RALSTON ♦
—VIRGINIA—
PRECISION CUTTING

Another cornerstone of Bram's system is bio-mechanical cutting. The reasons we use this concept are twofold: Through bio-mechanical cutting, we can eliminate the threat with minimal use of life-threatening force, and limit any, if not all, criminal or civil consequences.

Look at any number of modern knife fighting systems and you will see a multitude of powerful, graceful, and often lethal techniques—battle-tested and reliable, yet wholly incompatible with the modern sensibilities of society. Some will inevitably argue that it is better to be *"tried by twelve than carried by six,"* but one might have a difficult time finding a judge and jury who wouldn't be sympathetic to someone who has been blinded, scarred, disabled, or killed in a violent encounter. They might find it hard to believe that the injured person was the aggressor and that you acted responsibly and with restraint in defense of your life. So instead, we innovate in much the same way that Professor Presas modernized Arnis.

When Professor Presas began studying Arnis, the Filipino Martial Arts (FMA) were experiencing something of a decline. Part of the reason for this was that traditional training involved the defender striking the hand of the attacker with his stick, without the use of protective gear or armor. Professor Presas amended this so that contact was stick-on-stick, with the understanding that the hand was the target. In much the same way, Bram's method focuses on disabling the ability of the aggressor to attack by means of impeding the function of limbs instead of closing in and attacking the vital areas of the body and killing the threat. If the attacker was a car that was chasing you, you might think of bio-mechanical cutting as giving the car a flat tire.

Forearms: In this approach, the arms become the primary target, but we must now examine the relationship between form and function. At the forearm, we are concerned with the muscles on the inside and outside (or dorsal and ventral aspects). These forces act in two different directions and affect the grip. One force seeks to close the hand and the other, to open it. Bram describes the body as a hydraulic system interacting with a system of pulleys, weights, and counterweights. If the muscles on the inside of the forearm become compromised, then the grip releases and the fingers open because the force seeking to close them has been impaired. And, vice versa, if the outside of the arm is neutralized, then the grip closes tightly and will not open until acted upon by an outside force.

> **Biceps/Triceps:** Moving up the arm to the biceps and triceps, instead of the grip, we are now looking at the function of the elbow. If the triceps becomes compromised, the biceps take full control (as its force is unopposed) and the elbow bends and cannot be extended again. The inverse is also true: When the biceps are impaired, the triceps straightens the arm and it cannot be bent (remember the limitations of functional articulation? Bent or straight, open or closed).
>
> Now, if called upon to defend my life, when I am viciously attacked by Mr. (or Ms.) X, armed with that scary knife, I only need to use a small tool to disable their ability to attack, reach, and pursue me, so I can get to safety and call for help. This is also a far more relatable defensive method, as most people have cut their arms and/or hands in everyday life, as opposed to having had to inflict a life threatening or disabling injury. Thus, we have a core concept that provides effective and reliable life protection while limiting the chances of criminal prosecution and civil liability.
>
> —John Ralston

The Art of The Blade

XIII. THE REST OF THE STORY
Six Through Eleven

Up to this point, we have spent our time focusing on strikes one through five and twelve because these are by far the most common techniques in blade combat. In fact, a recent study suggests that the vast majority of knife attacks on the street come from a right-handed assailant either thrusting toward the stomach (#5) or slashing toward the face/head from the right (#1) or above (#12).

> ### HANDS OR FEET? LEFT OR RIGHT? STRAIGHT OR HOOK?
>
> A close quarters battle ("CQB") instructor once taught his recruits: If you do nothing else in a fist-fight, at least throw your left hand up. Why? Because most people punch rather than kick, and the majority of punches in a street fight are right-handed haymakers…

But once the practitioner is familiar with these core elements, there are still others to be considered, absorbed and employed:

#6 & #7 [v]: These ***sungkiti*** attacks are the second and third sides of the so-called "thrusting triangle" (#5→#6→#7) and target the region of the brachial plexus. Consistent with the principles of bio-mechanical blade-work, they will effectively shut down the arm on whichever side a successful attack is landed. Considering the legal—as well as tactical (blade suction, tip breaking…)—challenges, involving in stabbing, however, it is important to remember that the blade will also ***slice*** along this forward trajectory, producing ***"slicing thrusts"*** across any target it encounters;

#8 [ξ]: This series of forward rounding cuts ***(redonda)*** works best at close range, and is bio-mechanically best performed cross-body with the shoulder of the *non*-weapon side forward. This *Visayan*-flavored technique (like most of Bram's cuts) is angle—not target—specific, but, based on its characteristics, is often used against the wrist, without which, as we have seen, the opponent cannot even hold a knife, let alone use it. It is critical to cut to the *outside* of the live hand when performing this technique;

#9 & #10 [o]: These rising slices, which are best visualized as the upward parts of the **figure-8** form, target the hip and upper leg musculature, without which the opponent cannot stand, as well as catching any stray hand which might happen to be dangling in the vicinity!

#11: This cut tracks the same *(vertikal)* line as #12 but in the opposite direction.

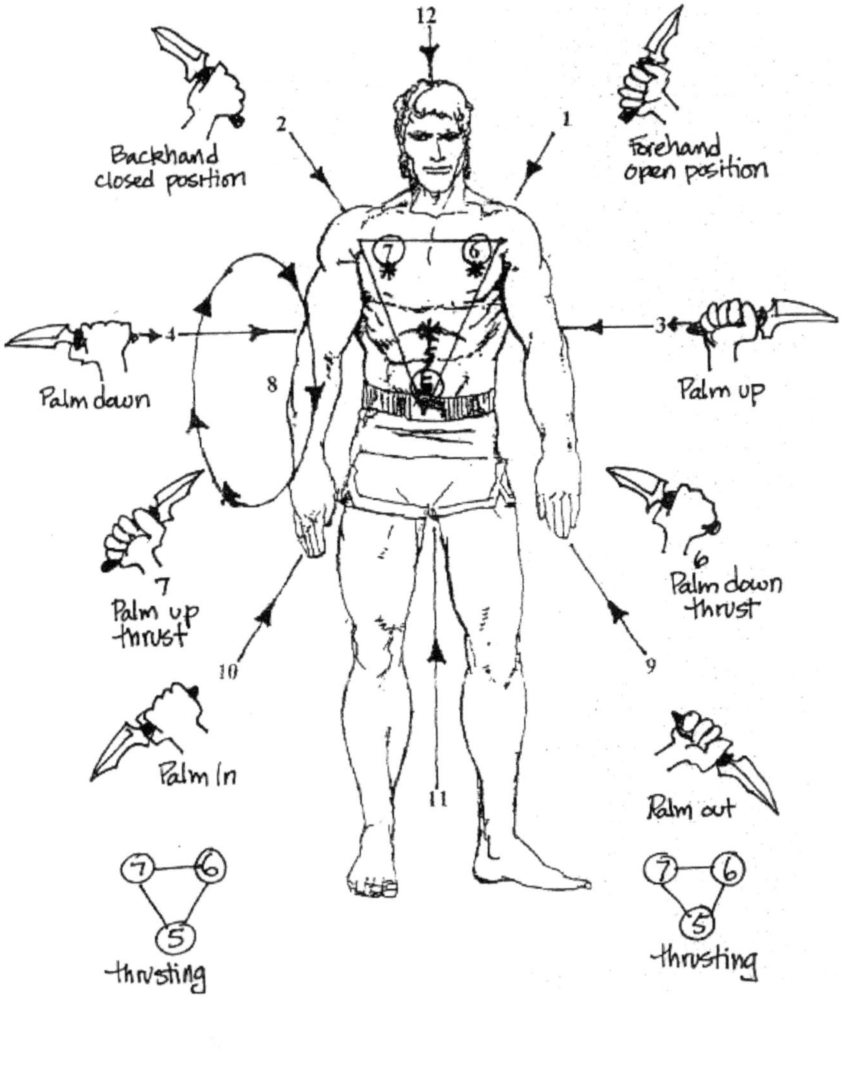

STIRRING

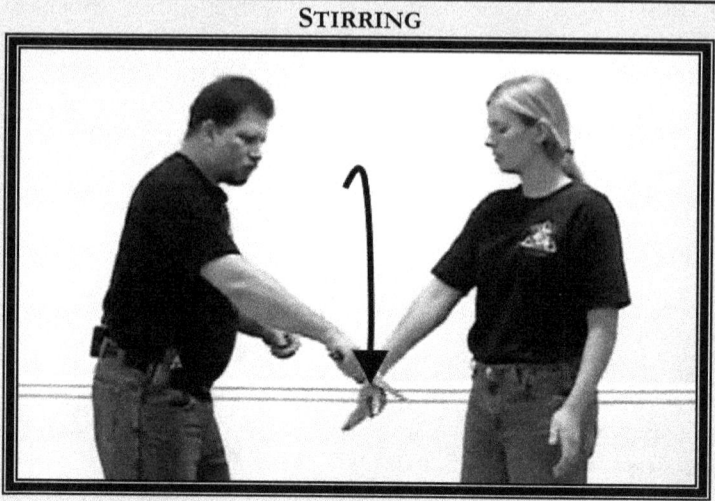

"Stirring" refers to using the tool (or hand) to redirect an attack (imagine that the blade is the ladle here and the pot is on its side). In this example, the opponent [R] has attacked #1, and the defender [L] has intercepted and cut inside the attacker's weapon hand/wrist, checked with his live hand, and then inserted his blade *outside* the attacker's weapon hand and used it to redirect the attacker's weapon down to the right and then back up to the left [in a clockwise circle] to re-position it. He can then grab/lock with the live hand and counter with the blade [#4].

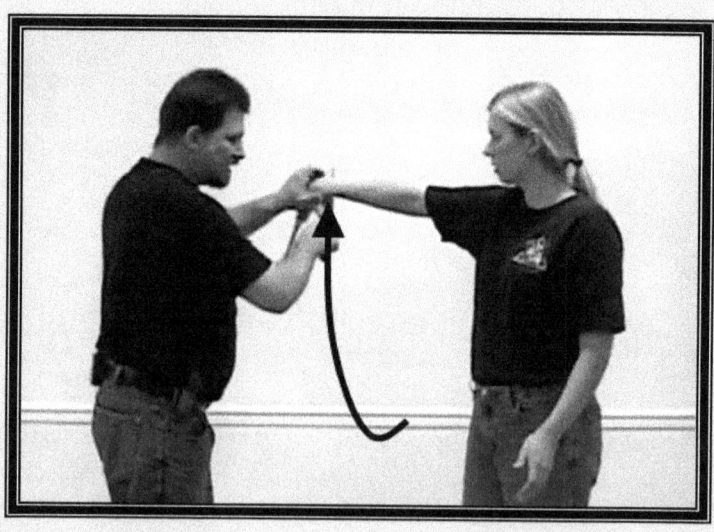

♦AMY KIRSCHNER♦

—IDAHO—

I met Bram twenty years ago in Palm Harbor, Florida. He was a guest instructor at the taekwondo school I was attending, and taught what I thought was stick fighting. I had no idea at the time that he would become so influential in my life, taking me to the other side of the world, visiting various countries and peoples, becoming a second dad to me, and teaching me how to connect to my inner confidence with his patience, art, and skill. It was even at one of Bram's seminars that I met my husband!

When I began training with Bram directly, he taught me flowing movements that were both beautiful and also made bio-mechanical sense. He often talked about what he'd learned from Remy Presas, and translated these lessons into material he taught to me (and others) in class. He studied, practiced, and combined several arts, always paying attention to detail. And when listening to Bram, you couldn't get enough of what he had to say. He always made everyone around him feel important. You always matter to Bram. He is loyal to a fault, and unfortunately, through the years, not everyone has shown him the same courtesy.

Common Sense Self-Defense/Street Combat isn't just a martial art to Bram; it's his way of life. The man eats, sleeps, and lives by a strict code of honor and discipline of movement. It's not just a martial art to me either. Thankfully, I was able to pick up CSSD/SC quite easily in the beginning, and it has only become more beautiful and more exciting as I continued to practice it. I find that I can feel the flows, the drills, and the movements. As Bram often says: "It's not brain surgery." Certain students I've encountered over the years tend to over-think it—tiny movements can be hard for some people.

CSSD/SC forces you to move, to notice, and to feel what is happening around you and to you. It doesn't employ big steps or massive motions; instead, it's about executing tiny, fluid movements—motion going with motion—from your hips, to your feet, to your shoulders. I enjoy it because it is an unexpected challenge and an empowered endeavor. In the martial arts world of big, tough men, Bram's tools and training are an equalizer—you don't need size and strength to learn his art and flow. When I first met Bram, I was an insecure and quiet teacher in my 20s. People scared me. But Bram, his art, and the people I have met along the way changed me and made me part of something remarkable. These experiences opened up opportunities for me to see the world through different eyes and view other people's perspectives. It was, and still is, an amazing adventure, even now. And this is all because of Bram. I will be forever grateful to him.

CSSD/SC is not only for big and strong men; it also empowers those who may feel weak. Paradoxically, women usually pick up the movements of this art most easily. This is so important because, due to their genetic make-up, women are usually the ones who need protection the most. At the same time, the simplicity and efficiency of CSSD/SC technique makes it a perfect choice for law-enforcement and the military. I even teach CSSD/SC to my own children, and bring them to Bram's seminars when I can. In all these cases, the basic movements become second nature to the students.

Another important aspect of CSSD/SC is that it uses purpose-built tools. Bram's knives are, in my opinion, simply the best. It is truly amazing when you consider how much time and effort he has put into perfecting these self-protection tools.

They are non-lethal, yet they can cut through layers of meat when needed. They are impact weapons as well as search-and-find tools. And they are made to be accessible and dependable under stress and duress, regardless of which hand is dominant.

Bram is a hero to me. He's someone who changes lives. In many ways, he saved my life. His lessons have enabled me to share with others how tiny movements could change or even save their lives one day. I can imagine no better teacher than that, and I wish him success in every way so that one day, everyone may see him as I do...

—Amy Kirschner

KITCHEN KNIVES

A fundamental rule of any martial arts practice is the more you train, the better you will perform (particularly under stress). And one of the best ways to increase results in this regard is to incorporate training into your daily life. As legendary master swordsman Miyamoto Musashi instructed half a century ago: *"Let your combat walk become your everyday walk."*

Among the many treasures that can be found in Bram's store is a set of kitchen knives modeled on his unique design. Given the frequency with which we cut all manner of items in our everyday lives, from shipping boxes to juicy steaks, these would be a welcome addition to any knife-fighter's kitchen. But the real opportunity for advanced training is not so much the specific blade as it is the cut. *Any* time you employ *any* knife for mundane purposes, you should pay close attention to the grip, the angle, the feel, and the motion. If you take nothing else away from this work, that concept alone can forever change your relationship with edged tools.

CROSS TRAINING

As a student of both Professor Remy Presas and Datu Bram Frank, I would like to share with you some key points of CSSD/SC that are central to the system and, in some cases, form the nexus of what Bram refers to as an opportunity to incorporate or transition to other martial arts.

Functional Limitations of Articulation: It starts with a simple concept. Any limb and/or joint only has three positions: straight, bent, or broken. With the elbow, a straight position can be illustrated as an arm-bar technique. An example of a bent elbow can be a chicken-wing technique. Finally, an example of broken elbow is the result of pushing past the anatomical limits of the supporting structures (e.g., bone, muscle, ligament, et al). Apply this concept to almost any technique in martial arts and take note of what part of the body is extended straight and what is folded. This becomes a solid foundation for pattern recognition and lends itself to learning transitions between techniques. Points of reference are critical to pattern recognition, especially while in motion.

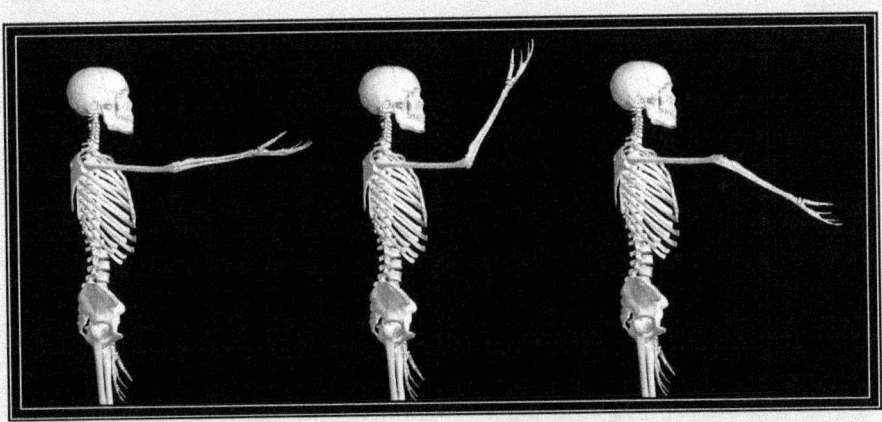

Angles of Attack—Blade vs. Stick: In the standard Modern Arnis curriculum for stick fighting, there are twelve angles of attack (initially, students should visualize these being performed with the right hand, but at more advanced levels, training will progress to encompass left-handed techniques as well). However, if we examine them through a lens similar to the one we used when analyzing the disarms, we can say that there are really only three angles of attack: Horizontal, vertical and diagonal. The variables that differentiate the twelve angles beyond these core characteristics are: The part of the tool that makes contact with the opponent; what position are we in; and in what direction are we moving the tool.

In terms of contact, we are either moving along a plane (e.g., cutting or leading with the edge) or poking (i.e., thrusting or leading with the tip); Positioning is either closed (i.e., your arms are crossed) or open (i.e., your arms are uncrossed); and with direction, you are either moving your tool from a high to low position, a low to high position or maintain equilibrium.

Using this model, we can break the twelve angles in standard Modern Arnis as follows:

1. Downward diagonal, along a plane, right to left, open to closed;
2. Downward diagonal, along a plane left to right, closed to open;
3. Horizontal along a plane, right to left and open to closed;
4. Horizontal along the plane, left to right and closed to open;
5. Thrust, lead with tip, to the midline and maintaining an open position;
6. Thrust with the tip from right to left and open to closed;
7. Thrust with the tip from left to right and closed to open;
8. Upward diagonal along the plane from left to right and closed to open;
9. Upward diagonal along the plane from right to left and open to closed;
10. Thrust with the tip on the highline from right to left and open to closed;
11. Thrust with the tip on the highline from left to right and closed to open;
12. Vertical strike along plane from high to low maintaining open position.

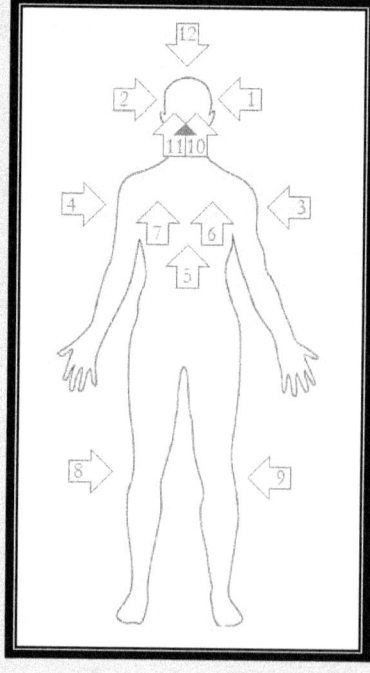

Many practitioners of Modern Arnis translate stick technique into blade technique literally, and this is easy to do until you realize the fundamental differences between the two weapons. Simply put, stick and blade are not interchangeable, nor are any edged and impact tools, even if their use employs similar vectors of motion. Accordingly, the angles of attack in Bram Arnis differ somewhat to reflect the differences between usage of edged and impact tools.

Angles one through five remain identical. Angles six and seven only change in as much as many practitioners using a stick employ something of a downward angle while thrusting. With an edged tool, the preferred method for penetration is tip angled up slightly. The common targets in both examples are the ribs of the attacker.

With an impact tool, you don't get much of a different result at either angle, but with an edged tool, when the tip is down, you will penetrate the skin with a 'tip rip,' but you are unlikely to penetrate past the ribcage without significant force (an edged tool differs from a stiletto or shiv in that the latter are stabbing tools designed to slip between the ribs). When the tip is angled slightly up as you thrust, you will find that the tip now catches and slices or separates the ribs and penetrates the vital organs, potentially causing significant damage.

An excellent parallel to this is found in Ryukyu Kempo as taught by Professor George Dillman: In Ryukyu Kempo, a three-quarter fist is commonly employed for many reasons. Among these is an understanding of how the ribcage inside the nipple line acts as a unit, and protects both the ribs and the viscera from the common full twist punch or even an uppercut. However, a three-quarter punch isolates the individual ribs, preventing them from functioning as reinforced unit, and rendering them vulnerable to damage and even breakage. Perhaps unsurprisingly, if you execute a #6 thrust, you will notice that your hand employs the same position as that required to deliver a three-quarter punch.

Angle #8 is a conceptual cut. It serves as a reminder of a vital principle. From the #7 position, you execute two elliptical cuts. This serves to illustrate or remind you never to cut forward with the live hand in front. From the stick fighter's perspective this is a perfectly valid movement. In Modern Arnis, we find it in single stick sparing drills and the Professor's earlier teaching of *tapi-tapi* (i.e., counter-for-counter); the movement itself is sometimes referred to as "bicycling." However, when using this bicycle motion with a blade, it soon becomes very apparent that you run the risk of slicing your own arm open, most likely at the biceps. Hence, the #8 cut illustrates a far safer method for cutting the bad guy and not yourself.

Angle #9 travels open-to-closed in an upward arc and angle #10 tracks the reverse trajectory. Together, they look like a reverse Figure-8.

Angles #11 and #12 are vertical movements. #11 moves from the low-to-high line, while #12 moves from the high-to-low line. While we do occasionally find a low-to-high vertical strike in many FMA, and even some Modern Arnis techniques, the important distinction here is that for the low-to-high #11, you rotate your wrist so that your thumb points down. This action pivots the blade, so the edge is towards your opponent and makes contact with the opponent. There is absolutely no benefit to running the dull side of the blade against your opponent.

—John Ralston

XIV. UNARMED DEFENSE
Disarming [π]

The majority of our studies to this point have involved *armed* combat. We now broach the subject of *unarmed* combat, but we do so *very* carefully.

In much the same way that the best block is: *"Don't be there,"* the only safe disarm is: *"Gently remove the weapon from your opponent's unconscious hand."*

Both of these somewhat jocular maxims have genuine tactical interpretations. In the latter case, it means that by far your best option is to defend in some other way that neutralizes or minimizes the threat—kicks to keep distance; bio-mechanical cuts to the wrist; knockout techniques—rather than attempting the *extremely* dangerous and largely fantastical feat of wrestling an edged tool from the opponent's actively resisting grip (if you don't believe this, try a full-speed disarm using a chalk or marker blade…).

Before outright dismissing the concept of empty hand against edged tool, it should be considered that the Modular defense to #4/#3 strikes involves just that, but it does so (a) using the bone-against-bone blocking method; (b) higher up the arm than the hand where motion is slower; and (c) only out of necessity.

Necessity is a valuable watchword in the realm of disarming. Just as kidnap-and-ransom specialists stress the importance of never allowing oneself to be taken to a secondary location, regardless of the risks inherent in resisting, so the decision to attempt a disarm should only be considered as a last resort. If—and only if—your attacker can't be evaded; can't be reasoned with; and can't be bargained with; then you may have to attempt this risky maneuver, but if you do, there are several mission-critical imperatives to be considered. With these disclaimers in mind, then, we proceed with extreme caution…

PRINCIPLE: DISARM WITH GREAT CARE (AND ONLY IF NECESSARY)

The good news—if there is any in this context—is that many of the techniques employed in knife-against-knife combat can be adapted for this purpose. For example:

† Where you would ordinarily intercept a highline slash (#1 or #2) with your blade, you can use your knife-hand to parry the attack.

† You are already accustomed to blocking low-line slashes (#3 and #4) with your bare forearm.

† And just as the umbrella block can be used to forestall an overhead strike (#12), so can the empty hand.

But just as mutual combat with weapons shaves down the margin of error as comparted with the hand-to-hand variety, so the armed-against-unarmed further raises the stakes. You really can't afford any mistakes at all. And chief among the most common errors—particularly with trained fighters—is overestimating your abilities and overcommitting to a plan of action.

The best approach is to keep distance until you are as sure as you can be under the circumstances that the time is right to counter. You must wear your opponent down, at least a little, so that he (or she) makes a mistake. In this regard, the following principles may be of some help:

1. **Expect to Get Cut:** This is likely to happen, so best to be both physically and psychologically prepared;

2. **Step/Shift:** The best block is: "Don't be there!" Step/body shift as in the blade-on-blade modules;

3. **Parry:** Your best ward is the intercepting parry—use a hand blade as in the blade-on-blade modules;

4. **Strike:** The best disarm is from a neutralized opponent; strike with your hand and cut with his blade;

5. **Kick:** While low kicks may be used to distract, they are not a viable way to disarm the attacker.

THE FEEL OF STEEL [τ]

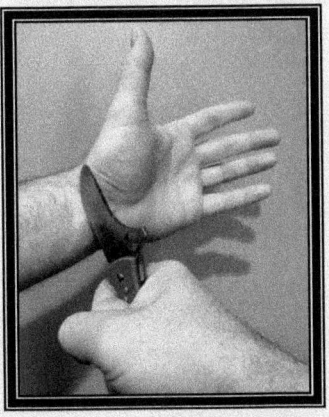

When you pick up a well-forged blade—particularly one that has been used in actual combat—you can feel something beyond the raw materials that make up the tool. There is an 'aliveness' to the metal; the sense of a slight vibration; as though if you were to close your eyes, you could actually hear the war drums and feel the rhythm of marching feet. There is a similar sensation when steel is pressed against your bare skin (even unsharpened). It's as though the blade is whispering, *"Oh, do I have your attention **now**?"* The serious, cold, relentless hardness certainly makes a powerful impression, and this can be used to great advantage when attempting to subdue an opponent, even without slicing ligaments and opening arteries. Any who trained with Remy Presas will recall the feeling of total control when the cane or blade is pressed against a vulnerable spot.

6. **Lock:** Once caught, the wrist can be locked to disarm in several ways (*kote gaeshi, sankyo, gokyo…*);

7. **Elbow:** The elbow moves at about one quarter the speed of the wrist, so it is a useful visual and tactile anchor point;

8. **Sleeves:** If the opponent is wearing a long-sleeved garment, the fabric can help augment arm control.

♦ JOHN RALSTON ♦
—VIRGINIA—
DISARMING

Nearly all disarming techniques use either a wrist throw position or a wrist lock position. In Modern Arnis, it is common to employ the standard striking pattern that includes twelve strikes and thirteen disarms (one for angles 1-11 and two for angle 12) based on your spatial relationship to the attacker's stick (e.g., whether you have zoned to the inside or the outside). However, all of these disarms result in the attacker being positioned palm up in a wrist throw (*kote gaeshi* or wrist-reversal) or a thumb down position (bent elbow wrist lock.) Disarms exploit the weakness of the grip. A strong grip requires the use of the opposable digit (thumb). The thumb is weak at either extreme of the wrist's limit of articulation. And the wrist throw and bent elbow wristlock are the extreme limits of articulation for the wrist. So, with this understanding, we can now say that instead of thirteen disarms in Modern Arnis there are really just two, and two disarms are a lot easier to remember than thirteen! Simplification—distilling a technique down to its essence—is essential to pattern recognition and discovering the foundational principles behind a technique. Principle-based training is a cornerstone of Bram's system.

♦ EDESSA RAMOS ♦

—SWITZERLAND/IRAQ—

I first met Bram while attending a World FMA Festival in Dortmund, Germany. The moment I saw what he did with the knife, I was instantly convinced that it was 'the real deal,' and that this was the grandmaster I must follow.

Before that, I had always complained that, while martial arts are good practice for the mind and body, as well as to preserve their precious legacy, in the real world they are rarely applicable. This is mainly because of the way they have been taught, especially during the last few decades, when martial arts practice got overtaken by profit-making motives, achieving fame and accolades, or the opportunity to travel the world for free if a teacher is able to get enough international students to sponsor him to visit their countries and teach in their dojos.

For too long, the martial arts have been associated with egotism, and there must be some basis to this association. Furthermore, many martial arts teachers who teach self-defense do not have enough understanding of the circumstances that put their students at risk, especially women. It is not enough to claim to 'know the streets.' It is imperative to know what violence really does, especially to women and everyone else who is vulnerable, and how that violence is deployed.

Out in the streets, in locations where violence is a reality and help is not readily available, a good teacher will want to make sure that the student is really capable of self-protection. Once you are cut, you cannot be un-cut. One you are attacked, you cannot be un-attacked. There is no going back. To be a victim of violence is like the BC/AD dividing line in history; nothing else is ever the same after that. I know this because I work with victims and survivors of violence every day. It is very important that fighting and self-defense techniques work in the real world. The risk of failure must be mitigated. Too much is at stake in a world where gender-based violence is a daily reality, especially for people like me, who work in perilous areas in some of the world's most dangerous places.

Therefore, in the martial arts, it is important to seek a teacher who exercises genuine commitment to the elimination of violence. Most of the time, the only way to do that is to fight. Effectively. And with no excuses. Bram is that teacher to me, and because of him, I am that kind of teacher to others.

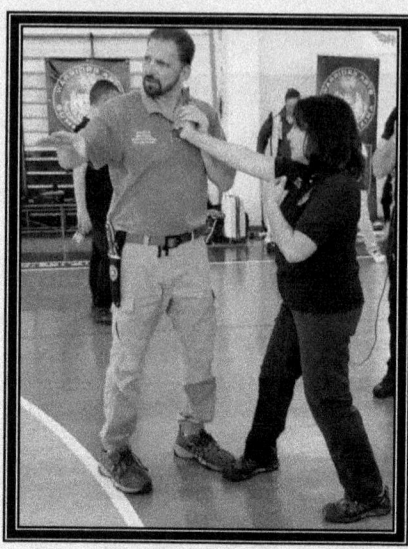

Arnis and the Filipino Martial Arts were developed by the Filipino people many centuries ago to defend themselves and their families, their homes and villages, from intruders, marauders, pirates, colonial armies, and all kinds of oppression. In the modern age, as FMA's popularity grew, and its practice spread exponentially, it is easy to lose some of the essential features of real protection and the real fighting art. While being adept with sticks and making impressive twirls is a feature of arnis, it is important for the practitioner to differentiate art, form, and exercise from the techniques that will really save one's life, most especially where a bladed tool is involved.

Disarming is a favorite feature of FMA. During practice, one can disarm the opponent, no matter what weapon is involved. There is no risk of death or injury if the technique doesn't work. One training partner is cooperative and compliant, for such are the rules of the dojo. And there is always room for improvement; one can always try and try again. But not in a real fight. Out in the streets, or in one's home, there is no way to control the context. It is impossible to predict which of many variables will play out. And there is no time. Decision, technique, and results must be decisive.

Bram taught me: *"Stick seeks bone; knife seeks flesh."* In many forms of martial arts training, the difference between an impact tool and a cutting tool is hardly explained at all. Training is a very forgiving context. It's okay to make a mistake; it won't kill you. It's possible to correct mistakes; the consequences are not life-threatening, not in a training hall.

The most important thing I learned from Bram is the concept of "biomechanical movement"—to work with the human anatomy, to move your limbs and hands and feet in a natural sequence, the way the human body was designed to move. It is not necessary to spend decades learning to push the body to its limit, to employ stances that are impossible to achieve otherwise. If you carry a knife, or if you can acquire one when you are about to be attacked with a knife, you cut. There is no killing involved, for cutting is calculated to achieve one true purpose: Disabling the attacker's knife hand. Preventing the attacker from being able to run after and catch you. And if necessary, destroying the attacker's ability to see you. It is the best self-defense because you get the desired result: safety, without killing.

Bram's 1-4-12 sequence follows the classic Filipino fighting concept of *depensiba-opensiba* (defensive-offensive). It is simple and effective. It has to be simple. The truth is, during a fight, most people are not really able to react quickly, evaluate myriad techniques, make fast decisions, and choose the right moves to execute, especially if fighting is not their profession or daily preoccupation.

I have demonstrated the effectiveness of Bram's training method and all the sequences he has put together many times. In addition to police and soldiers, I also teach women and girls. It is the ordinary women and girls whose safety are of the most concern to me, especially in a place like Iraq (where I work), in refugee camps, where women are most vulnerable to gender-based violence, and in the villages where they have no protection. When I teach them 1-4-12, 1-2-2, and 2-3-12, I see that spark of understanding, that "aha" moment, as if a full bright light is suddenly shone onto their darkness. It is the beginning of their journey to real self-defense.

Even though the sequences are relatively easy to learn, developing true proficiency requires training and many repetitions. Training is required in order to tune the mind, to make it present to the moment, and to develop the heart and will to use one's knife with intent and save one's life. Training is also important in order to un-learn certain tendencies, especially if the martial artist has trained for a long time in sticks and empty hand, or in grappling and boxing.

When attacked with a knife, the usual tendency is to block with the empty hand, as if to protect the hand holding the knife, or to clear a path for the knife-hand to deploy. This is very dangerous and it doesn't work. You will get cut for sure, and once you receive that first cut, the shock and pain of it might render you incapable of fighting and further defending yourself. Your knife is your weapon and your shield, your defensive and your offensive. Learn to deploy it as your first move, always.

The Art of The Blade

The *sumbrada* is one of Bram's most important signature moves. *Sumbrada* is an excellent technique in Filipino martial arts. It comes from the Filipino-Spanish word "sombrero" or hat. The weapon hand can be deployed repetitively, over and over again, without having to change stance, angle or position. The weapon hand circles around the head, like fixing a hat, and goes immediately for the follow-through strike. You can keep your arm close to your body while doing so, making the technique suitable for close-quarter fighting. It is a classic FMA move developed by the Filipino masters many centuries ago. Not only is it a great training pattern, it is one of the best real fighting techniques.

I have known Bram for eighteen years now. His system has many more techniques, far beyond the collection of sequences that he is best known for. I've spent time with him, traveled with him, assisted him and co-taught with him. Some of the most potent learning moments I've experienced were not even in the training hall—like one time in Venice, eating pizza, and drawing techniques on a table napkin! Bram is also the one who taught me the art and joy of eating sushi, and that those are moments that are perfect for discussing techniques, asking questions, challenging assumptions.

I have had many grandmasters in my studies, and I honor and learned from each and every one of them (such as the late Grandmaster Cristino Vasquez, Bram's Filipino brother). But it's Bram who gave me the most cohesive view of the fighting arts; a constellation that works not just for me but also for so many others who truly need it. And a constellation that is not exclusive, for it welcomes all other martial arts knowledge into its cohesive view. *"Make the art your own."* Grow it. Use it. Share it.

—Edessa Ramos

XV. BRINGING A KNIFE TO A GUN FIGHT
Never Underestimate the Blade

PRINCIPLE: NEVER UNDERESTIMATE THE BLADE

While many would consider a firearm to be more dangerous than an edged tool, Bram disagrees, putting the knife at the very apex of the lethality pyramid. This is so for several reasons:

First, a gun only projects force in *one* direction whereas a blade can threaten in *any* direction. As a result, if you get out of the direct line of a muzzle, you will probably be relatively safe, at least momentarily—with a blade, not so much.

Second, handguns are far less ubiquitous, accurate, and easy to employ than Hollywood would have you believe. Knives, by contrast, are far more common and intuitive tools (can you think of any household that doesn't have a knife somewhere in it?). The chances of running into an assailant armed with a gun who can and will actually use it effectively are not high.

Third, the physiological and psychological effects of being cut with a blade can in many ways be more devastating than a simple bullet wound. In fact, merely brandished a blade can have a devastating effect on the intended victim.

The Tueller Drill: In the early 1980s, a police sergeant in Salt Lake City—Dennis Tueller—conducted an experiment to determine how fast an assailant with a knife could reach and attack a target twenty-one feet away. Before you take a guess, keep in mind that this is about the distance between the sidewalks on either side of a standard two-lane crosswalk.

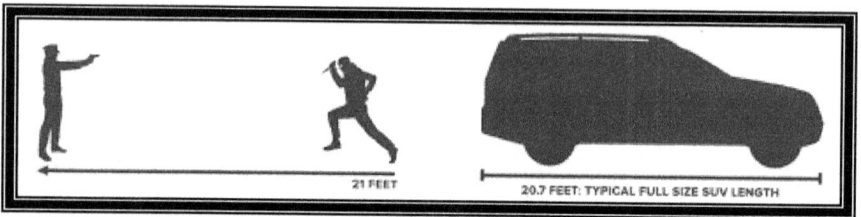

The answer is 1.5 seconds. That's about two heartbeats. And that is a frightening statistic, especially for patrol officers.

The next logical experiment, then, was to determine how fast a typical police officer could draw, ready, aim, and fire his sidearm. Even under ideal conditions, the answer was often not within the second-and-a-half that the blade-wielding attacker needed to reach and dispatch his victim. This well-publicized finding gave rise to the so-called '21-foot Rule' in law enforcement training circles, describing the zone of danger for officers on patrol.

> **MYTH BUSTERS**
>
> In 2012, the Discovery Channel series *Mythbusters* attempted to replicate this experiment and found that under ideal conditions, the gunman was able to shoot a knife-wielding attacker at a distance of **twenty feet**, but any closer and the blade found its mark before the bullet did.
>
> Bram, however, notes that the shooter's goal should not just be to hit the attacker, but to displace him, and, in that case, the true safe distance is closer to ***thirty-two*** feet.

This drill can be set up in a number of ways, but the more realistic, surprising, or stressful, the configuration, the slower the gunman's reaction time and the larger the corresponding danger zone. According to Bram, his military and law enforcement students confirm that this is the case. And the inevitable conclusion is that in most indoor settings—and a good many outdoor encounters as well—the knife may in fact be a more effective weapon than a gun, at least a holstered one.

Like everything in the arts, though, this too is a matter of balance. While underestimating the blade can be dangerous, so too can focusing on it to the exclusion of all else. In other words, as Bram explains, just because someone has a knife, doesn't mean you should forget your other tools.

THE MONKEY'S PAW

In some countries, wild monkeys are a valuable commodity for a variety of purposes. Among the ways trappers catch these quick and clever creatures is to place an attractive food item in a jar whose mouth is wide enough to reach in with an open hand, but narrow enough to prevent withdrawing the contents using a closed fist.

Rather than having the sense simply to let go of the bait and move on, monkeys will often remain 'trapped' for hours or even days until the hunter returns, all because they refuse to let go of their prize…

The lessons to be learned here are:

One: Respect the blade, but don't allow yourself to become hypnotized by it. Remember you have hands and feet with which to work as well.

Two: Remember that the key to your way out is often in your own hands (or feet).

And Three: Don't be a monkey!

MODULAR GUN

> ### IT IS ALL THE SAME!
> One of the most compelling aspects of Modular is the way that it applies across weapons systems. Bram integrates firearm ergonomics (old sword ergonomics) into the use of the blade and bolo. This way, when you learn to use <u>one</u> tool using the Modular system, you are in fact learning to use <u>many</u> tools. In the end, as Professor Presas used to say: *"It is all the same!"*
>
> —Bruce Chiu

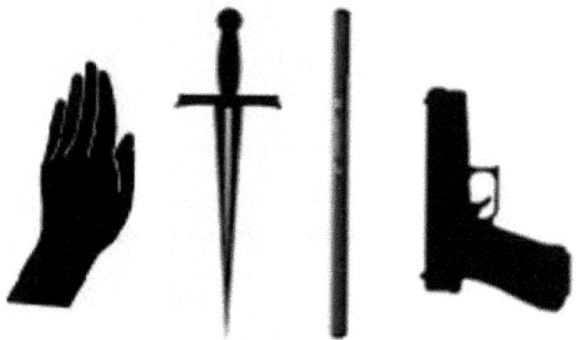

Some of Bram's students who carry firearms for a living teach modular gun techniques alongside his modular knife system. Given the obvious differences between 'edge' and 'point' tools, however, it is remarkable how many tactical and strategic concepts these two systems share:

1. **<u>Ensure Safe Access</u>**: Holsters should be oriented to allow for drawing easily and quickly *without* crossing your body.

2. **<u>Do No Harm</u>**: A good place to begin in any weapon system—but especially when dealing with a tool that can inflict so much damage with so little effort—is avoiding inadvertent injury.

When it comes to firearms, this means:

(i) Keep the muzzle pointed in a safe direction—ideally down—even when you and/or the weapon are in motion;

(ii) Keep the weapon close to the body and hold with a straight wrist;

(iii) Keep your index finger off the trigger until ready to fire; and

(iv) When firing one-handed, keep the free hand (and other body parts) out of the field of fire.

3. **Biomechanical Shooting**: Like bio-mechanical cutting, bio-mechanical shooting is based on a hierarchy of body system functions (nerves, tendons, muscles, bone, and blood in that order). Unlike the fictional firefights commonly shown on film, people who have been shot often continue to function for minutes or even hours unless they have been hit in one of only a few "instant shutdown points." In fact, studies suggest that many times people only fall down when shot because that is what television has taught them is the appropriate response!

System Shutdown Points:

(i) The triangle formed by the eyebrows and nose;

(ii) The head of the femur;

(iii) The spine.

Regional Shutdown Points:

(i) Arm: Brachial plexus/shoulder/clavicle;

(ii) Forearm: Elbow;

(iii) Leg: Knee.

| STEEL SEEKS FLESH, WOOD SEEKS BONE, POINT SEEKS JOINT |

4. **Body Shifting**: A corollary to the weapon safety protocols described above is that the best way to turn the weapon is to turn the body. In addition, as a 'point' weapon, a firearm is primarily dangerous in a single direction. Accordingly, the best defense is to shift off the firing line, and the best offense is to keep your target on the firing line.

5. **Respect/Fixation**: While it is vital to respect every weapon, it is important not to become fixated by its power. Even when you are carrying a firearm and your opponent is not, there are still many dangers to be avoided.

6. **Deployment/Disarming**: As evidenced by the *Tueller* drill, having a gun, and being able to use it to stop a knife-wielding attacker, are two very different things. Realistic expectations regarding reaction times should be taken into consideration and the muzzle should be directed downward not just for safety reasons, but also to facilitate a 'pull-back and shoot' defense from an attempted disarm (which likely won't work with the weapon directed upward);

7. **Impact Tool**: While using a firearm as a club may seem like a colossal waste of technology, the harsh reality is that at close range, it is likely a more effective way to use the weapon than trying to discharge it safely and accurately. And once in this unenviable position, modular knife concepts like intercept-check-counter, rigid blocking, and many other techniques illustrated by the give-and-take drills work surprisingly well.

It should be noted, however, that while such forceful contact is unlikely to lead to accidental discharge, it may cause a firearm—particularly a semiautomatic handgun as opposed to a revolver—to jam or misfire. For this reason, 'drive back' shooting is preferred to impact shooting or contact shooting (and Bram is working on an attachment for handguns that will avoid this unwelcome side-effect).

8. **Aftermath:** In addition to the myriad concerns that must be taken into consideration when using a knife in combat, unique to firearms is the extent of the lethal range of its projectiles given the ease with which bullets can punch through targets and continue travelling on a potentially lethal trajectory (a mile or more depending on caliber and conditions).

♦ JOHN RALSTON ♦
—VIRGINIA—
UNDERESTIMATION

A core principle of Bram's system is never to underestimate the power of edged (and impact) tools.

A stick offers several tactical advantages, including increased range, force multiplication, and mechanical advantage, as well as the potential for use as a lever. The benefit of employing an impact tool is that the tool feels no pain when making contact with the target, whereas fists might. For these, and many other reasons, impact tools should never be discounted as valuable weapons of self-defense.

Edged tools share many of the same benefits: They extend range, feel no pain, create mechanical advantage, and can be used as impact tools to some extent, either while closed or by employing the butt (Bram's blades are actually created with a spectrum or continuum of uses and applications in mind). The obvious difference is that an impact tool requires more strength to employ than an edged one.

Empty hand defense requires more strength than impact tools as well, but edged tools do not rely on strength. Rather, they rely on sharpness, edge orientation, and the duration of the contact with the attacker (the greater the duration of the edge contact, the longer and deeper the cut).

This ties in very nicely with the Small Circle Jujitsu principle of sticking, control, and sensitivity. In addition, edged tools not only require less strength to employ, they also mitigate or even neutralize the strength of the attacker. If an attacker presses forward and the defender places steel to flesh with the edge maintaining contact, the forward pressure ceases until the obstacle of the blade is removed. In most cases, this will result in retreat, with the attacker grabbing his own bleeding arm, and possibly finding that he cannot open his hand (since you have employed bio-mechanical cutting). Of course, there are exceptions to the effectiveness of this technique, such as drug usage and extreme emotional states, and these are variables that should be considered before committing to an action prematurely.

> **PUNCH THROUGH**
>
> An advantageous corollary of this phenomenon, however, is that shutdown points on your target can be reached by shooting *through* various bodily obstructions, leading to 360-degree bands of vulnerability (around the head/neck, chest, and hip) rather than just surface targeting. This is especially helpful when used in conjunction with drive shooting, as the opponent who is driven back is likely to be contorted in one way or another, potentially obscuring familiar surface targets.

XVI. ARMOR
Defensive Equipment

For as long as there have been bladed weapons, there have been defenses against them. Beginning with the body's own natural structures—which inform target selection—warriors have constantly sought to improve defensive equipment for repelling attacks. Leaving aside shields for a moment, this equipment has usually taken the form of some kind of armor.

While the days of chunky chainmail and polished steel breastplates are behind us, modern warriors of all kinds still employ helmets, chest protectors, and even gauntlets and shin guards in some situations. Accordingly, those who study the bladed arts must consider how such defensive equipment impacts their practice.

In recounting military exercises in which he was required to teach tactics to soldiers facing opponents with considerable chest protection, Bram observes that imperatives like mobility will always create weak points in the defensive shell which can be exploited to good effect. Places where protective materials must give way to more flexible joints—the collar, the hips, the wrist, and so on—will always be good targets.

♦ BRUCE AND CHRIS CHIU ♦

—FLORIDA—

First Meeting (Bruce): It's so interesting—I don't actually remember first meeting Bram—it seems like he's just always been around. But I guess as longtime students of Professor [Remy Presas], he and I must have initially crossed over on the seminar circuit sometime in the early 1990s. Whenever Remy introduced people who he obviously cared about, they instantly became family, so Bram and I never really had to go through a period of feeling each other out; we just hit it off from the beginning. If ever people the Professor cared about didn't get along, it really hurt him. And I know that the Professor had a special place in his heart for Bram. I remember once when Bram released a book on Modern Arnis, someone asked the Professor if that was okay. He responded, *"Anybody else, no, but Bram, yes!"*

Legacy (Chris): As the son of a grandmaster, I was fortunate to grow up with an extended family of amazing martial artists around me from before I could even walk. It wasn't until the last few years, however, that I really started training in earnest with Bram. Having trained in Modern Arnis with my father, I asked about Bram's skills, and my dad confirmed that Bram is 'the real deal.'

Heart (Bruce): Bram is so passionate about his art and his students. A wise master once said that a great teacher gives of his soul, and so it is with Bram—it's not a case of, *'you are what you do,'* but rather, *'you do what you are.'* Anyone who has met Bram knows that the most amazing thing about him is the size of his heart. I remember one particular seminar when I was going through a tough time personally. Bram came up to me, and without trying to placate me or condescend to me in any way, he simply looked me in the eye and said with total sincerity: *"If there's anything I can do for you, just let me know..."*

That's when I knew we would be brothers forever. Bram is such a genuine guy, and can be so loving and generous that it even works to his detriment at times—over the years, some people have taken advantage of those wonderful qualities in him…

Titles (Chris): I was raised to use my teacher's titles when training with them as a mark of respect (in Bram's case: Grandmaster), but, as many of you know, he doesn't stand on ceremony, and tells everyone, *"Just call me Bram."* For me, however, the solution was simply to use the respectful appellation: "Uncle Bram." I remember Bram once saying to my father, *"I wouldn't do stick against you because you would beat me up,"* and my father responding, *"I wouldn't do knife against you because you would cut me up!"* Their mutual respect was clearly evident, and what a great environment for a young martial artist to grow up in.

Teaching (Bruce): Bram can talk about his art for hours without taking a break, but unlike many people who have only academic knowledge, he can also back it up in practice. He has developed an effective and powerful standalone system. Having been in the arts for many decades now, I have witnessed the way in which his skill with the tools and his ability as an instructor have grown exponentially over the years. It's simply mind-blowing the way he can extrapolate blade techniques effortlessly from the lessons the Professor taught us and also effectively convey them to others. And in many ways, he brought the Professor's art full circle: The Professor translated from the blade to the stick and Bram brought it back to its bladed roots.

Blade Work (Bruce): Some people don't even know that Professor Presas taught knife work, but one thing that anyone who was paying attention can tell you is that he always said that if you can do something with a stick, you can do it empty-handed, and you can do it with a blade. A stick *punyo* can be a knife *punyo*, can be a hammer-fist, and so on… And there were many clues along the way. For example, he always used to say: *"If I touch you, you are cut already!"* It's just that some people were too blind to see this.

Bram tells people he's been trying to get me to use his knives for almost thirty years, but when he finally put one in my hand, it just felt right. Bram says I smiled like it was Christmas, and adds, *"That's when I knew I finally got him!"* [or as my son Chris said recently, *"Maybe you've been a knife guy all along…"*]. And one last thing in this regard: Don't let Bram tell you he can't do stick—he is extremely proficient on that side of the house as well!

Curriculum (Chris): Based on the approach taken by these great masters, when a student asks me about our knife curriculum, I always say, *"We don't have a knife curriculum."* When they ask about our stick curriculum, I say, "We don't have a stick curriculum." When they ask about our empty-hand curriculum, I say, *"We don't have an empty-hand curriculum."* Don't overcomplicate it. As Professor used to say, *"It is all the same."*

The Journey of a Lifetime (Bruce): There's an old joke: How many martial artists does it take to screw in a lightbulb? The answer is three: One to do the job and two to tell each other, *"That would never work on the street!"* But seriously, if you have been doing the martial arts for more than, say, five years, it's likely not because you're afraid of getting attacked on the street or because you're trying to get into shape—you stick with it because you love it—it's the journey of lifetime. In this regard, Bram truly makes practice fun and his love of the art comes through loud and clear.

The Dark Arts (Bruce): For ethical and moral reasons, the Professor did not like to teach deadly techniques. He used to say, *"If two men fight with knives, there is only one outcome."* Bram has continued to honor that tradition by developing systems (like bio-mechanical cutting) and tools (like the CRMIPT) that are designed to be less-than-lethal. While Bram and I sometimes teach specialized skills to military operators, there is a sharp dividing line between what we will share with law-abiding civilians versus those who engage in potentially deadly combat for a living. In this regard, Bram truly lives and works on 'the bleeding edge.' He knows the pulse of the community. He is in tune with the time-tested techniques as well as the latest innovations in this arena—heck, he's even developed many of them!

Disarming (Bruce): Bram always says that your chances of disarming a knife-wielding attacker with your bare hands are slim at best, and I agree with that whole-heartedly. In fact, my preferred way to disarm an attacker is by taking the blade out of his unconscious hand! One of the things I learned when dealing with special operators, is that if you are out-gunned (or in this case, out-bladed) and retreat is not an option, *attack immediately*. In other words, if you have no way to escape, you are far better off launching a full frontal assault and trying to knock your opponent out before removing his weapon from his hand.

There are three dynamic elements of combat: Target, weapon, and movement. If the opponent has a weapon and you don't, you better pick another target and move on it! And the best way to do this is with speed, surprise, and violence of action. These three elements create chaos, and we can capitalize on that chaos, especially if we are the ones to create it first. We know that while the human brain can work through pain, it can't work through chaos. These are fundamental elements of what I teach.

Knife Against Gun (Bruce): When it comes to the Tueller drill, I agree with Bram that people tend to underestimate dramatically what constitutes a safe distance. Remember: When people run these tests, everyone knows that an attack is coming. The average cop on the beat has no such warning. And in the artificial environment of this drill, in addition to knowing that an attack is coming, the subject often knows the identity and starting position of the attacker—luxuries which the agent in the field does not have. If you truly want to gauge the parameters of safe distance in this realm, try having multiple potential attackers, in multiple locations, so as to inject at least some element of surprise into the equation. In this scenario, the only option is often to strike first (before attempting to draw your weapon), and/or use your sidearm as a blunt-force deflection tool.

Armor (Bruce): As a former law enforcement officer and an occasional military trainer, I also agree with Bram's assessment that modern body armor does not render the blade ineffective. There is simply no operationally-effective way to armor the entire body, and there is also no physical way to make armor flexible enough for realistic use without having vulnerability at the joints. From a historical perspective, many *Daito-ryu jujutsu* techniques are based on attacking the weak-points in traditional *samurai* armor. And without saying too much, this exact vulnerability is why law enforcement agencies have adopted a more forward-facing shooting stance in recent years. In my opinion, the best blade target is any skin you can see (and there will always be some) because if something is blocking your view of the skin, you have no idea what kind of barrier it may conceal.

> **Tapi-Tapi (Bruce):** I was there when Remy first introduced Tapi-Tapi. In the parking lot after that seminar, somebody asked if it could be done with a blade, and everyone replied, "Bram can do it!" Sure enough, he did! The way Bram does Tapi-Tapi with a knife illustrates how Modular can be used as a method for teaching Professor Presas's Modern Arnis.
>
> **The Future (Bruce):** Through my son, I have recently re-connected with Bram and some of my other colleagues from the old days who I haven't seen in person for quite some time. As luck would have it, after moving around for years, I finally settled in Clearwater, less than a mile from where Bram lived when I first met him. I drive past his old house almost every day. And even though he has since moved considerably further south, Chris and I visit and train with him from time-to-time. In fact, we have another trip planned when the pandemic finally lets up. It will be great to see my brother and train with him again.
> —Bruce and Chris Chiu

Finally, while in modern times shields (unless of the improvised variety) only tend to be used in specialized situations, like riot-control or bomb-disposal, it is worth considering that holding a shield fully occupies at least one hand and also tends to reduce both agility and visibility for the user.

XVII. THE SWORD
Bolo & Katana

While this book—and Bram's workshop as well—are primarily concerned with shorter blades, the principles of Modular apply equally to longer edged weapons, like the *bolo* [Q] or even full-length swords as well. Having learned at the hands of Professor Remy Presas, Bram is no stranger to making or working with these farther-reaching tools.

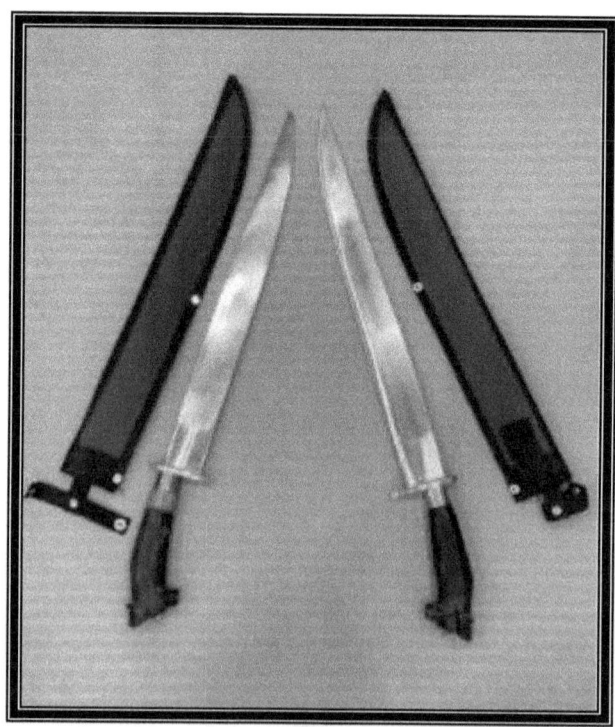

Of course, the added length of these 'elder brother' tools changes range calculations, but unless your opponent is using a knife against your sword, the distances involved will still be equal, and most of the operating parameters (exploiting range, body shifting, bio-mechanical cutting, etc...) will remain proportionately constant. One longtime student of Bram's art—Jason May, who is also a senior exponent of *Musō Jikiden Eishin-ryū Iaido*—has conducted an in-depth exploration of the way in which the designs, principles, and practical techniques of the Filipino and Japanese blade arts converge and combine.

♦ JASON MAY ♦

—COLORADO—

THE RAZOR'S EDGE NEVER LIES

My initial introduction to Grandmaster Bram Frank came through studying his art well before I actually met the man himself. Some years ago, while under the instruction of another great teacher of Filipino Martial Arts—Guro Chad Bailey—I first became fascinated with, and later influenced by, Combat Arnis and the Modular System. Embedded within the curriculum of Guro Bailey's Progressive Arnis are various extensions of *sumbrada* from the Modular System (with all their unique trademarks intact).

Prior to commencing these studies, however, I also had the privilege of studying *Iaido* under M. J. Sullivan Sensei (*Seiho*). With great respect to all the masters I have been influenced by, it is my intention to affirm the effect of Grandmaster Bram's teachings in enhancing my *Iaido* practice.

Initially, Guro Bailey challenged me by refining each motion of the *sumbrada* drills I was familiar with from other Filipino systems. The tedious repetition was a credit to Guro Bailey, who had learned from Grandmaster Bram's obsession with delicate precision. As a razor's edge never lies, Grandmaster Bram's approach captured my attention, just as *Iaido* had years before. In confronting the difficulty required to execute Modular System drills, I quickly saw why it holds its place with good reason within the vastness of the Progressive Arnis curriculum.

Guro Bailey added to the mystery of Grandmaster Bram with stories of his contribution to the martial arts community and his propagation of the Modular System within various police agencies and military forces. Wanting to push my comfort level and satisfy my peaking curiosity, I decided to attend a Bram Frank seminar and test my level of understanding of Modular System concepts under his watchful eye. Unbeknownst to me, my perception of technical necessities, timing, and oddly enough, my skill within the Japanese sword begin to evolve.

During my first Modular System seminar, I became keenly aware of Grandmaster Bram and his ability to draw attention with his famous "foam noodle" demonstration. As much as I appreciated his real-world experience applying bladed technique, the approach Grandmaster Bram took in applying 1-4-12 *sumbrada* with a knife left me questioning my own technical prowess and understanding of timing. The basis of *sumbrada* learned years before was grounded in the *largo* and *medio* (long and medium) styles of movement. Grandmaster Bram's perspective, however, occurred at *corto* (close) range, which immediately challenged my initial interception of attacks and ability to adjust my footwork quickly.

Prior to my introduction to the Modular System, I was fortunate enough to study various other martial arts: I have experienced the staunchness of traditional styles and flexibility of collaborative systems in their various flavors and tones. After the first Modular seminar, I saw the relationship of strictness in concept *combined with* flexibility in timing within Bram's system.

While practicing finding my 'flow' and being 'in the moment,' I realized that I could combine multiple facets of the martial arts in such a way that it did not jeopardize tactics or principles. The sharp yet caring tone of Grandmaster Bram during this first seminar provided me with another source of humility and a bridge to a new perspective.

Progressing in confidence with the concepts within Modular System, I began to note improvement in my timing and accuracy. More importantly, the cognitive process through which I thought about the bladed arts was also developing. A familiar sense of angles with a formula for detecting probable counter-attacks gave rise to an immediate urgency to rediscover my own internal framework. Bridging the gap between traditional Filipino *sumbrada* stick drills and the use of bladed instruments became essential in developing a variety of timings for handling uncomfortable scenarios. Repetitions of drills in right-handed and then left-versus-right seemed to present more questions than answers. Trusting intuition in exploring all timing patterns and determining how I could best command the battlefield became my new-found objective.

The influence of Grandmaster Bram and the Modular System certainly did not end with my study of Filipino or Indonesian martial arts. As a practitioner and teacher of *Iaido*, classical approaches to instruction taught by my teacher M.J. Sullivan Sensei *(Seiho)*, began to mold and shift my focus. The long-standing modality of teaching and understanding angles and range within *Musō Jikiden Eishin-ryū Iaido Seiho-Ha* (The Only Direct Tradition of the Eishin School of Drawing the Sword, Seiho Clan)[1] allowed me to identify similarities in hand position and edge use in the Modular System.

Examining Grandmaster Bram's Folding Katana blade revealed biomechanical principles behind the design shared with the old country-style *Eishin-Ryu Iaido* cutting techniques predominant in *Iaido Seiho-ha*. The old country-style of drawing which I learned focuses the centerline on the target (versus turning the centerline as with the All Japan *Iaido* Federation style—*Zen Nippon Iaido Renmei*). The common approach of covering the centerline provides power from the pivoting of the feet and hips within the Modular System and explosive power in the *Seiho-ha* style of drawing from a seated position *(seiza)*.

---

[1]. This, and many of the other technical terms and descriptions referenced herein, may be found and further researched in: Sullivan, M. J., <u>Sword and Psyche: Hachigenri and Other Writings on the Martial Arts</u> (Double Dragon Press, 2001).

Investigating further revealed several more points of crossover between these conventionally separate arts. Grandmaster Bram's Folding Katana knife shares both elements of subtle design and mechanical methods of deployment in slicing and thrusting with *Shinogi-Zukuri* sword work. The point of the Folding Katana blade is classified as straight-edge (*fukura-kaeru*)[2] with a small size point (*ko-kissaki*) by traditional Japanese sword-making standards. The straight edged point is meant to keep the draw within the framework of the body while intercepting the opponent at the shoulder and finishing the cut on the opposite side of the torso, as the small tip operates without being burdened by too much depth. In applications for thrusting, the small tip allows for quick penetration and retraction, providing an advantage especially if fighting multiple attackers.

The *Shinogi-Zukuri* design was the most commonly used shape from the Heian period to the end of the Edo period (794 AD to 1868 AD). Although *Musō Jikiden Eishin-ryū Iaido* is credited as beginning in the Muromachi Period (1384 AD to 1574 AD), the *Shinogi-Zukuri* design predates the Muromachi period. As the only carryover from the Heian period, the *Shinogi-Zukuri* sword design has a ridgeline and is over two *shaku* (1 *shaku* equals 11.93 inches) in length. Grandmaster Bram's Katana shares the same *Shinogi-Zukuri* ridge line with a "Bramp," as an impact tool and kinetic opener, combining functionality and battlefield ingenuity.

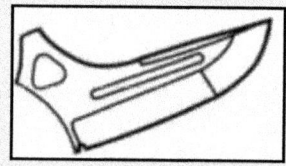

The relationship between the depth of curvature (*zori*) of the common katana designs like *Shinogi-Zukuri* (with ridge-line) are consistent with the Folding Katana blade design as well. The drawing cuts of Modular System are applied at close quarters and long range as needed for engaging and successfully cutting a target with precision. Similarly, the methodology of drawing and cutting within *Iaido Seiho-ha* in the first set of techniques known as *Seiza no Bu* (Formal Sitting Group) apply to close range engagements while sitting in the court of a *daimyo* (feudal lord), while longer range attack scenarios dealing with standing and running engagements as within *Tachi Uchi no Kurai* (Situations for the Long Sword) are comparable to the *medio* range of Modular System using shorter edged weapons.

[2.] This, and certain other material referenced herein, may be found and further researched in: Yumoto, John M., The Samurai Sword: A Handbook (Tuttle Publishing, 1958).

Shared by both arts respectively, the Modular System and Iaido operate mechanically within macro and micro levels of drawing, cutting, and thrusting. The macro level of cutting and thrusting shares attributes found within the first foundational *waza* of *Iaido Seiho-Ha* known as *Mae* (Forward), which utilizes the small shape tip (*ko-kissaki*) to aid in a fast draw known as *Koi Kichi no Kuri* (cutting the mouth of the carp).

The engineering of the small tip, depth of the curvature and shape of the scabbard (*saya*) all aid in preventing the practitioner from cutting through the scabbard and the hand. Upon successfully drawing, the opening cut follows the path of backhanded slicing similar to the Modular System, followed by a downward arc cutting motion of the overhead angle.

Similarities at the micro level are exhibited within the development of hand dexterity and grip. As practitioners are taught in *Iaido*, the horizontal and overhead cuts begin by elevating the *iaito* (practice sword) ninety degrees by gripping pinky-to-thumb to create the largest base of a cutting motion. Through the extension of the arc, cutting occurs as the hands "wring the towel" (as Sullivan Sensei would often say), while indexing the second row of knuckles amplifies the magnitude of the slice. Once the cut is complete, the sword is pushed out and away at a forty-five-degree angle to push the opponent's body out of the way. The push of the sword is led by the indexed knuckles of the right hand as it prepares for a purging of blood from the sword (known as *chiburi*).

Similarly, the design of the Bramp on virtually all of Bram's blades offers a pistol grip which utilizes the indexing of the second row of knuckles for fast deployment and centerline drawing. The relationship to the old country-style of drawing seen in the Modular System lends to ease of kinetic opening.

The functionality of the Folding Katana blade design mimics the horizontal and vertical cuts of the first four *waza* of the *Seiza no Bu* and *Tachi Uchi no Kurai* respectively, by indexing the knuckles and extending the wrist. The combination of indexing and extension allows for the creation of space to dominate the battlefield and protect the centerline. Although the vertical and overhead cuts within *Iaido* and the Modular System vary in the size of their arcs, the principles carry over regardless of disparity in weapon length, and converge in the study of macro and micro dynamics.

The influence of Grandmaster Bram and his Modular System have most certainly pushed my understanding of the technical aspects of the bladed arts to deeper levels of study, but the psychological approach I was taught in both arts remains the same. Developing physical attributes and stillness of the mind (*zazen*) are to be unified and maintained at all costs. The purpose of unification is to enhance the response to external threats, allowing the internal spirit to do the same. In answer to the question: "Why study the martial arts?", I find the conclusion to be that this practice utilizes tangible tools to sharpen the mind, body, and spirit in alignment so as to be truly present in the moment and recognize 'nothingness' (*mushin*).

Through the teachings of Grandmaster Bram, I have discovered tools to enhance my warrior mind, body, and spirit in order to discover the void that is *zazen*. Realizing the connections between the Modular System and Japanese swordsmanship, I am humbled to train my heart and spirit as one, as exemplified by the words of the master swordsman Miyamoto Musashi:

"To attain the Way of strategy as a warrior you must study fully other martial arts and not deviate even a little from the Way of the warrior. With your spirit settled, accumulate practice day by day… When your spirit is not the least clouded, when the clouds of bewilderment clear away, there is the true void."

—Jason May, *Kyoshi, Musō Jikiden Eishin-ryū Iaido Seiho-Ha*

XVIII. LESS-THAN-LETHAL
The Aftermath

> **PRINCIPLE: ALWAYS CONSIDER THE AFTERMATH**

The saying: "Live to fight another day" has at least two components: The first is the directive "live," with which the majority of the material covered to this point has been concerned with. But the second is: "to fight," which is a hard thing to do from a jail cell or the poor house. Students, and especially teachers, of the Art of the Blade should carefully consider the life-changing effects of criminal and civil liability—both direct and vicarious—before picking up a knife. The most brilliant technique is useless if it results in criminal or civil liability. And, as previously discussed at length, the goal of the Modular fighter—to inflict the minimum amount of injury necessary to defeat the threat presented—is in lockstep with the applicable criminal and civil legal standards governing the use of force in the modern era.

LETHAL TECHNIQUES

Lethal Techniques: There are many ways to kill with the knife, including: Puncturing the skull, cutting the spinal cord, and slicing arteries (or veins). There are even more ways to maim, including: Severing limbs or digits, slitting open internal organs, disfiguring and blinding. Bram and his instructors certainly know these kinds of highly dangerous techniques, but they do not teach them, at least not to civilians, and not in public.

No.	Name of Artery	Size	Depth below Surface in inches	Loss of Consciousness in seconds	Death
1....	Brachial	Medium	½	14	1½ Min.
2....	Radial	Small	¼	30	2 "
3....	Carotid	Large	1½	5	12 Sec.
4....	Subclavian	Large	2½	2	3½ "
5....	(Heart)	—	3½	Instantaneous	3 "
6....	(Stomach)	—	5	Depending on depth of cut	

Fig. 112

Rather, as we have seen, the Modular system, and the blades specifically designed for it, are designed to disable an attacker *without* causing death or permanent injury. Cut the flexor tendons and the opponent cannot make a fist. He cannot hold a weapon. He cannot grab. He probably can't even turn a doorknob. And while this kind of injury is far more serious than a bruise or a superficial laceration, it can be repaired.

This kinder, gentler approach to edged tool self-defense is important for moral, psychological, and legal reasons. And while morality alone should be a sufficient basis for considering this way, more self-serving considerations also militate in favor of adopting this approach. The toughest street cops and the most battle-hardened soldiers admit to those they trust that acts of extreme violence—whether given or received—haunt them for years or decades to follow. And zealous prosecutors and aggressive plaintiff's attorneys will be more than happy to point out any potentially less injurious path that might have reasonably been followed.

CLOSE RANGE/CONTROL RESPONSE MEDIUM IMPACT TOOL (CRMIPT) [c]

The tool-maker in Bram has taken this new thinking a step further when it comes to law enforcement:

What use is a knife that has *no* sharp edge and *no* point?

When that tool is made by Bram Frank and used by law enforcement officers, the answer is: Plenty. Keep two things in mind:

† The law favors the use of non-lethal methods whenever possible; and

† Bram's tools have a wide variety of uses beyond cutting and thrusting.

Accordingly, Bram's CRMIPT, color-coded blue, retains the following features when closed:

1. **Ergonomics:** The pistol grip—in combination with other ergonomic aspects of the tool's design—enables powerful, intuitive, gross-motor, grabbing and gripping using the web of the hand and also parallels firearm lock activation/visual confirmation;

2. **The Bramp:** Which allows the tool to be used as an impact weapon for pressure point striking and a flesh or fabric grabber.

3. **The 'Teeth':** This 'jimping' on the ramp, the lock-release, and elsewhere facilitate grabbing and trapping of flesh and cloth;

4. **The 'Horns':** These deliberate outcroppings at various points on the profile also facilitate grabbing and trapping of flesh and cloth;

5. **Indexing:** Depressions in the handle and clip are designed to allow for controlled grip transition;

6. **The Ambidextrous Clip:** Which allows it to be oriented comfortably according to personal preference and varying hand dominance;

7. **Seat-belt Cutter/Window-breaker:** This specialized feature has myriad uses over and above those for which they are initially intended.

And when opened (manually or kinetically using the Bramp):

8. **An Unsharpened, Rounded Edge:** The shape and size of this retractable edge extends the user's reach and also allows him (or her) to direct and control a suspect with a variety of techniques. Some of these are similar to those employed with a *kubaton*, with the added advantage of a thinner surface area, concomitantly resulting in the ability to apply greater pressure with less force.

♦ TOM AND ED ♦

Tom Gallo — Ed Frawley

Tom Gallo and Ed Frawley are longtime friends, accomplished martial arts teachers, and die-hard New Yorkers. They both grew up in the arts— Ed studying traditional *karate* in the Bronx from the age of nine, and Tom following the path of *Hwarang-do* as a young man (and later developing interest and expertise in the Filipino Martial Arts). A chance encounter at a trade show in Florida in 1994 served as Tom's initial introduction to Bram Frank. At this event, Bram was demonstrating the then-unreleased CRMIPT, and, based on the way this tool was working on Tom's instructor at the time, he knew right away that it was something he wanted to add to his martial armamentarium. He eventually shared his interest with his friend and colleague (Ed), who immediately became fascinated with this unique and innovative device.

Over the years that followed, and assisted by various technologies, from old-style VHS tapes to modern Zoom training, Tom and Ed continued to train with Bram, eventually earning instructor certifications in the use of the CRMIPT. This is not the full extent of their Modular training, or indeed their overall martial portfolios (In addition to *Hwarang-do* and FMA, Tom has also trained extensively in *Chen Tai Chi* and *Silat*, and is a certified *Kyusho* instructor. When Ed's first instructor moved away, he transitioned to *Goju Karate* and then especially *Seido Karate*, along with some boxing, FMA, and *Kyusho* training), but in talking with them, it becomes clear that the CRMIPT, both in design and application, is something they have truly, and enthusiastically, come to love.

Living in New York, these gentlemen are well aware of the heightened restrictions on everyday carry weapons, and it is in this context that Bram's preference for the term "tool," and the non-lethal features of the CRMIPT are so important. There is a huge difference between being caught carrying a knife on the street, and transporting a less-than-lethal rescue tool to or from a legitimate martial arts training hall. And lest anyone think that the CRMIPT is somehow less effective as a tool of self-defense, Ed and Tom can correct that assumption with years of training and teaching with this specialized device.

Right away, beginners can be shown how to employ the CRMIPT like a ball-peen hammer while closed, striking at vulnerable points on the hand, wrist, arms or body. While this action is easy to understand, Ed adds a subtle teaching nuance: Many novices tend to choke up on the tool, almost like they are afraid of losing it, whereas relaxing and lowering the grip allows it to be deployed to best advantage. Ed even keeps a small hammer in his school to allow students to see and feel the correct way to perform this fundamental technique.

Like any tool, however, there are certain other actions that require practice to perform correctly. Two that Tom points out right away are pivoting—that is, using the handle indexing to move from forward to reverse grip without losing one's grasp on the tool, and "the Pac-man move"—holding the tool in a half-open position and repeatedly snapping it shut in a "snipping" manner. Both men agree, that the best way to get proficient with this tool, however, is to handle it a lot. Practice, practice, practice, and carry it with you everywhere that is permissible.

In talking with Bram's colleagues and students, two main points connect all the conversations like a golden thread: The man is a brilliant martial innovator and he has a heart as big as all of the outdoors. Ed and Tom agree unreservedly on both counts.

Tom says: "Bram is a very exacting instructor; he expects us to get it right. But he is also the most generous teacher you could have. He's always willing to share everything he knows so freely," to which Ed quickly adds: "Tom and I have worked really hard and I'm proud that Bram is so pleased with our progress. But really, I'm even prouder to say that we have all become such good friends. Bram really puts his heart into everything he does, whether it's teaching, designing, or friendship. There's no one quite like him."

The Art of The Blade

IXX. COMMANDMENTS OF STEEL
Life and Death Matters

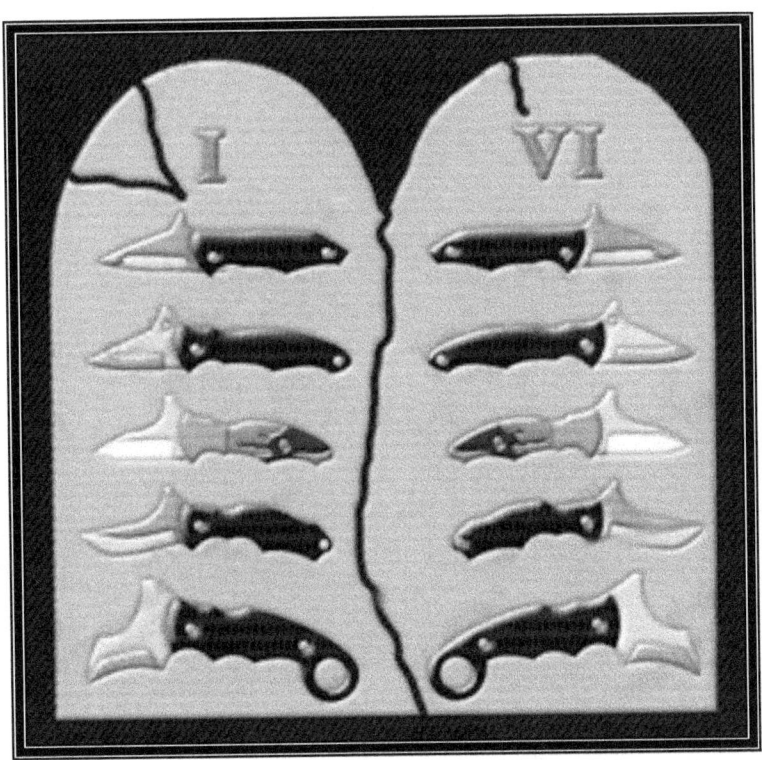

When it comes to matters of life and death, a strong case can be made that those who live in nations at war have the best perspective. The armed forces of Israel have been in a state of almost constant conflict for over a century (at least since the 1917 Balfour Declaration). Accordingly, their martial arts have been well tested in the crucible of combat.

Dr. Dennis Hanover—a martial arts pioneer and gold-medalist recognized as a Tenth Dan by the OEJJU, and holding high *dan* rankings in many different arts—instructed Israeli Special Forces for decades and developed a counter-terrorist program *(Lochama B'Terror)* that has been in use in that country since in 1987. Suffice it to say that Dr. Hanover understands the application of real-world martial arts in a way that few others can.

When Dr. Hanover first met Bram in the mid-nineties, they instantly recognized each other as kindred spirits, and became fast friends and frequent training partners. Over the years that followed, Dr. Hanover often sponsored Bram to come to Israel and teach his bladed art to elite military units and security agencies. And one of the aspects of Bram's system with which Dr. Hanover was most impressed was the Commandments of Steel, and awarded Bram dan/instructor ranks in his personal atrial arts system.

> We have a great bond in the way of the blade and great respect for each other in the martial arts. I see [Bram] as the first knife instructor in Israel and one of the finest in the world. I wish [him] health, happiness, and an interesting life. May [he] go from strength to strength.
>
> — Brother and friend, Dr. Dennis Hanover

As discussed, the Modular System is reality-based and common sense-driven. Having taught his methods for decades to combat soldiers, law enforcement officers, and security personnel all over the world, Bram knows better than most the grim reality of life and death at the edge of a blade. As a result, his system is predicated on—and tested by—a number of foundational principles.

If you learn nothing else from this book, copy (or cut out) this page and pin it up in your school or *dojo*.

Commandments of Steel

I. Steel cuts flesh, *always* [corollary: Wood crushes bone];

II. You cannot change the First Commandment: You don't have to like it, but you do have to deal with it in combat;

III. Unless you are Superman, the First and Second Commandments *always* apply: In other words, there is no point trying to find a way around this fundamental truth;

IV. The principal of a knife (an edge that cuts flesh) has never changed: For millions of years, this is what knives have been designed to do and what makers and users have striven to perfect;

V. Lead with the edge, thrust with the point: Use the parts of the blade for the purposes for which they were designed;

VI. Grip is determined by range, range is determined by length: How you grip a knife depends on where your hand is relative to the opponent. The longer the weapon the greater the range, the shorter the weapon the closer the range;

VII. Disarming an opponent who has a knife is unrealistic: The only one who is likely to be disarmed (quite literally) is you;

VIII. Weapon accessibility is paramount: By far the worst tool for any job is the one you don't have;

IX. Using steel is deadly serious: As with firearms, never deploy a blade unless you intend and need to use it, and can live with the aftermath;

X. One fighter drips, the other gushes (or sports a toe tag): Or, as the old saying goes, if two tigers fight, one bleeds and one dies…

♦ JOHN RALSTON ♦
—VIRGINIA—

Bram understood and utilized the importance of principle-based training for nearly all of his Modern Arnis journey. As a direct, lifelong student of Professor Remy Presas, he was exposed to the teachings of Professor Wally Jay (including the Ten Principles of Small Circle Jujitsu). This had a significant impact on Bram. Professor Jay's Principles became a core tenet for him as he incorporated Small Circle Jujitsu into his application of all martial arts. Any martial art that does not include those principles will be enhanced exponentially by exploring how they might be incorporated.

In the mid-1990s, Bram began teaching internationally. While in Israel, he introduced the **Ten Commandments of Steel** to students. The Commandments are the fundamental tenets of Bram's core philosophy regarding the use of edged tools for self-defense.

Commandments 1 through 4 exist to counter the mythology of Hollywood-style martial arts. You are not going to catch a blade by clapping your hands together. You are not going to block a blade with your empty hands. You are not going to kick a knife out of a knife fighter's hand. Simply put, your hands, blocking arms, and your leg will be cut. No matter how many people claim, *"But, I've done that in a fight,"* the odds are that the attacker was either uncommitted to inflicting harm, untrained, or both. Grandmaster Ed Lake would often remark: *"You do not train to handle the 90-percent of people who don't know how to fight. You may not need to train to defend yourself against them. You train for the 10-percent who know how to fight and are willing to hurt you. The 90% are easily handled then."* An edge exists for the sole purpose of separating matter. A knife held against you, or being used to threaten you, is not fulfilling its purpose.

Commandment 5, edge orientation, is paramount. Many examples of this commandment have been mentioned previously. Review them to gain a better understanding of how important it is.

Commandment 6 reinforces that you should not train exclusively with one grip. Learn how to use both effectively and transition between grips and ranges. Do not have an expectation of what grip you will use in defense of your life. The edged tools Bram Frank designs and produces factor in escalation of force, moving from control to impact to live-edge deployment, as well as having attributes to aide in grip changes while under stress.

Commandment 7 also means that being disarmed is more difficult than the novice imagines. Bram spends considerable time on weapon retention and counter disarms in the Modular System.

Commandment 8 is often overlooked and not just with edged tools. Instructors will often run into a person who relies on pepper spray, their keys, something on their key chain, or even a concealed firearm. The question to them always should be, *"How often to you carry it in hand? How often do you practice with it? How often do you practice deploying it?"* We all know physical skills are perishable. Training must be consistent to be practical.

If you rely on a tool for your protection, there are additional factors to consider: The tool's quality, maintenance, and your ability to reach and use it under stress. Think of the *samurai*, who mainly practiced the draw and primary cut with the katana. Do not assume you will just get to it when you need it.

Another practical issue arises when we consider what happens during a sexual assault. If you keep your edged tool in your pants pocket, and your pants are pulled down, the tool may no longer be within reach. For this reason, those wanting to defend against sexual predators may want to keep a second folding edged tool somewhere more accessible, like inside a bra or shirt. Where pants may be unreachable, a shirt or dress may be left in place or moved by the attacker and therefore be closer to the hands of the victim making it still within reach.

Commandments 9 and 10 are both self-explanatory. They should reinforce Commandments 1-4. If an edged tool is used against you, treat it accordingly. The differences between unharmed, maimed, or dead can be a fraction of an inch. Prepare, train and remain vigilant. Never believe it can't happen to you.

—John Ralston

<u>Certification</u>

Bram's MBC^2 system is not the only approach to bladework—but as those who have contributed to this work have revealed, it is an extremely powerful one on a number of levels. If you agree, the next step may be to seek training from the founder himself, or any of his authorized instructors. They provide teaching and certification in this art in a number of forums, including an online component, which is particularly helpful when—as now—our world is in a state of lockdown.

Basic Instructor
Common Sense
Self Defense / Street Combat
Modular Blade Concepts: Martial Blade Craft

The above named person is recognized and certified as a
Basic Instructor
in the conceptual art of CSSD/SC MODULAR MBC²
Modular Blade Concepts: Martial Blade Craft

Within the art is Presas Arnis, Modern Arnis, & Combat Arnis. This art is based / founded on the art of Modern Arnis founded by Professor Remy Presas. It involves and contains elements of JKD, Wing Chun, Dennis Survival Hisardut, Small Circle JuJitsu, American TKD / karate and Aikido. This art of CSSD/SC modular has been designed and innovated by Grandmaster Bram Frank and it contains the use of Kinetic and Full force continuum tools designed by GM Frank. CSSD/SC MBC² and CSSD/SC Arnis are officially recognized as a style of martial art by the WHFSC. All warriors in this art of CSSD/SC must exhibit honesty, loyalty, common sense, honor, respect, dignity, understand might for right, fight injustice, defend the constitution, protect the weak and must defend the rights of the people against the use of tyranny and abuse.

Death Before Dishonor : Skill is Rank

The Art of The Blade

XX. MAKE IT YOUR OWN
Forms, Patterns, and Dimensions

Like his own teacher, Remy Presas, Bram encourages students to absorb the fundamental elements of his system and then adapt them to their personal preferences and proficiencies in order to *make the art their own.* For example, one student with a background in the traditional Japanese martial arts—who was often forced to train alone during the global pandemic of 2020—created a solo form to practice all four of the core modules *seriatim*, and a letter system to help remember various patterns.

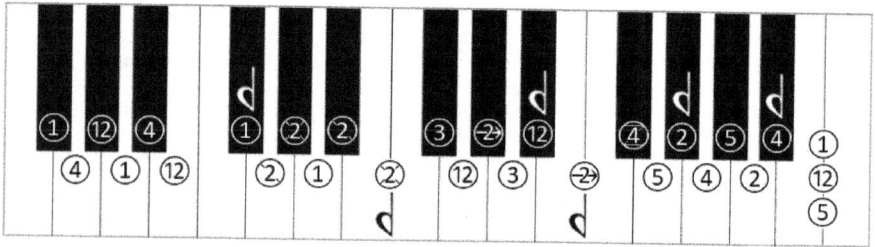

1. **Solo Form**—when performed solo, the practitioner 'plays' the 'white notes' while visualizing the opponent 'playing' the 'black notes.' In keeping with the noblest martial traditions, the opponent strikes first (#1).

2. **Repetition**—By repeating each module twice, the practitioner has the opportunity to perform both sides of the form before transitioning to the next one.

3. **Decision Points**—places where the practitioner or the opponent must choose to switch to the next module—are indicated by the letter: "d."

4. **Switch Points**—Where the practitioner encounters a barrier and has to change tack can also be inserted.

5. **Shape Cuts**—Mnemonic devices designed to help remember certain check-and-cut combination trajectories [L-cut, 7-cut, X-cut, etc…].

♦ BRIAN ZAWILINSKI ♦

—CONNECTICUT—

I first met Bram at one of the many Grandmaster Remy Presas Modern Arnis seminars hosted by Sifu Richard Roy in the late 80s/early 90s in northern Massachusetts. Throughout the 90s, Sifu Richard would host the Professor for seminars in May, late July (the East Coast Modern Arnis Summer Camp), and periodically a seminar in the Fall as well.

Bram was already off and running on his own outside of the Professor's events, whereas I was traveling and following the Professor whenever/wherever possible to keep learning as much as I could from him. I started working in the prison system in January 1992 and I found Modern Arnis (in conjunction with my eleven years of Kenpo at the time) to be a priceless addition to my "toolbox" due to its close range, diverse mix of techniques, locks and takedowns, etc.

As we all know, we lost the Professor on August 28, 2001, but the training, seminars, and camps continued. Fast forward to July 2006: I was invited to teach at FMA III and the Remy Presas Modern Arnis Memorial Camp in Tagatay, Visayas, Philippines (two-week program). I knew my other "Unka," Dan Anderson, was going and I was traveling with none other than Roland Rivera.

We got to Tagatay on day two and after a few hours of chaos and mix-ups in accommodations, we found ourselves at the Taal Hotel and who do I hear has arrived? "Unka" Bram. Since I probably hadn't seen him in 14+ years, we had much to catch up on. We spent the next two weeks doing so, and since then, everyone mentioned thus far has remained very close. There were several others present to include Dieter Knuttel, Bambit Dulay, Rene Tongson, Rodel Dagooc and the late Cristino Vasquez, all of whom (apart from Cristino of course) I remain in touch with to this day.

We trained at a different location almost every day within a one to two-hour drive from the hotel. This included a massive shopping mall (Mall of Asia?). They blocked off an area on the ground floor for us—we were about seventy-five people deep—and it was directly underneath the open atrium air space in the floors above us. Several of the top tier instructors were tasked with teaching at this location and while I was teaching Empty Hand *Tapi Tapi* (half of which is literally Trapping Hands and the other half is a modified version of the same), all of a sudden I heard this "heckler" yelling down from the floor above to some of the folks I was teaching: "You know this, this is our High Line Drill!" I ignored the voice, but it persisted, and I eventually looked up and see it was Unka Bram! He came running up to me right after that session and told me he had never seen anyone teach that drill in that manner other than him (only he teaches it with steel . . . go figure). Rest assured, I watch carefully whenever Bram teaches, not only for the content, but for his modular method and approach which is very interesting.

Just about a year later, I hosted the first ever "Sticks 'n Steel" seminar with Bram in Middletown, Connecticut. During this seminar, Bram found out that he had been admitted into the *Black Belt Magazine* Hall of Fame as Weapons Instructor of the Year. It was pretty cool to watch his face light up when he got the news.

I've been in close contact with Bram ever since, and to both his and Dan's credit, they worked me over for about six years to get me to openly accept and use the title "Grandmaster" with a much broader brush stroke than I was currently using. Bram was definitely the lead instigator and Dan was his backup! The efforts were sincere and selfless; Bram stood to gain nothing other than the satisfaction of dragging me into a brighter spotlight for the road and years ahead. It was a matter of getting me to see the bigger picture and in his words, "to take my rightful place at the table."

This effort peaked in Omaha, Nebraska, in 2015 with my stepping in front of a council of elders (which included Bram) with none other than Dan by my side as one of my ukes. Dan was originally supposed to be a guest on the board itself, but last minute politics squashed that arrangement so I "countered" the situation by bringing him in as an extra uke. I wanted Dan to be present, but ultimately, I did not intend for him to partake in the exhibition. I almost pulled it off until Bram said, "Hey what about Dan!?" As God is my witness, you can't make this stuff up! I had no choice but to have Dan participate, but thankfully, most of the heavy-handed work was already done.

> The exhibition was extremely well received and we were literally stopped at the exit on our way out with handshakes and accolades. As crazy as it played out, I wouldn't have had it any other way. Yet another chapter in the history of Modern Arnis and a testament to the selflessness and dedication of GM Bram Frank! I am blessed to have Bram in my innermost circle. *La Familia!*
>
> —Brian Zawilinski

THREE DIMENSIONAL THINKING

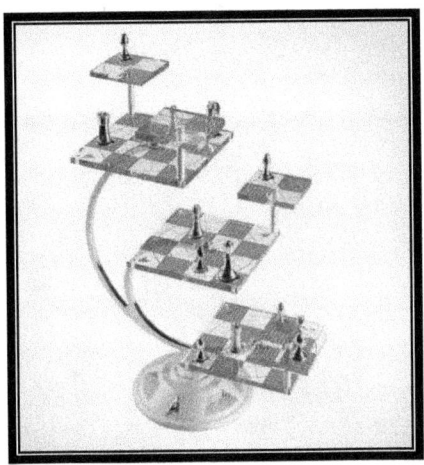

Just as that there are only so many ways that the human body can move, there are also only so many spatial dimensions through which an attack can travel—three to be precise: Side-to-side strikes (x-axis); up-down blows (y-axis); and backward-forward thrusts (z-axis). One of the many brilliant things about the give-and-take patterns is that in these brief exchanges of attacks and counters, defenses along every possible axis are employed.

In addition, with a little fancy hand and footwork, the practitioner can transition smoothly through these dimensions while simultaneously switching from cane to blade to empty-hand and back, using almost exactly the same pattern for each method. When perfected, it makes for a stunning showpiece and a powerful cross-spectrum training tool.

XXI. THE WORDS OF THE MASTER
Bram Frank

✛ **Basic Movement:** The basic design of the human body has never changed, throughout history, and this what I based my system on. Unless something bad has happened, we all have two arms and two legs. And these limbs only work in certain ways. Your arms are hinge mechanisms and can only be open or closed—there are no other choices.

    1. Following: Open right to open left; [can start either hand]
                              Close right to close left.

    2. Alternating: Open right, close left;
                              Open left, close right.

    3. Weaving: As in Modern Arnis *Sinawali*.

→ **Modular System:** I designed the Modular Blade Combat/Concepts system to stand the test of time. By using primary building blocks (red, yellow, blue, black, white), it allows different practitioners to arrange them in different orders to suit personal preference, while everyone is still using the same pieces. There is no need for anyone to split off in order to change the system, because the ability to change is already built in. In this way, if I were to come back and visit this planet in a thousand years, it is my hope that I would still see people practicing this art and still recognize the pieces.

In the Modular color scheme, the primordial shades—white and black—represent the grips and perspectives respectively. In the primary palette, red evokes the bold strokes of the foundational 1-4-12 drill; yellow signifies the transitional 1-2-2 form; blue stands for 2-3-12 and purple for 5-2-4. In the secondary palette, orange—the blending of red and yellow—denotes switch points, and green (yellow and blue), decision points.

What truly makes the system modular is that it is comprised of different modules which are all linked by one or more common elements. For example, the practitioner can use the #1 strike in 1-4-12 to transition to 1-2-2, and the #2 strike in 1-2-2 to transition to 2-3-12 or 5-2-4. The order of the numbers within any module is where strike becomes the closest counter.

Time Shifting: The ancient masters identified certain core attributes of the accomplished warrior, including the strength of the tiger; the speed of the serpent; the agility of the leopard; the grace of the crane; and the wisdom of the dragon. But what if you had to choose just one of these? A moment's reflection makes it clear that the choice must be speed, since all the strength, agility, grace, and wisdom imaginable cannot be employed against a target which cannot be caught, and, reciprocally, no matter how tough the target, wave after wave of lightning-fast strikes will eventually wear it down.

Many survivors of life-threatening situations—military combat, crime victimization, natural disasters and the like—report that in the heat of the moment, everything seems to slow down around them, giving them plenty of time to analyze and deal with the situation; in a relative sense, giving them the gift of enhanced reactive speed. This documented phenomenon is known as: Tachypsychia.

TACHYPSYCHIA—THE CORE OF THE ART

Tachypsychia is a neurological condition that alters the perception of time, and is usually induced by physical exertion, drug use, or a traumatic event. It is sometimes referred to by martial arts instructors and self-defense experts as, 'the Tachy Psyche effect.' For someone affected by tachypsychia, time perceived by the individual either lengthens, making events appear to slow down, or contracts, with objects appearing to be moving in a speeding blur. It is believed that tachypsychia is induced by a combination of high levels of dopamine and norepinephrine, usually during periods of great physical stress and/or in violent confrontation.

Would you believe that there is a way to summon this ability to alter the apparent flow of time so that the opponent appears to be moving in slow motion? Would you further believe that students of the classical arts have been practicing this skill for years, most without even knowing it? Developing this power involves several different, but interrelated concepts:

1. **Focus**: At the beginning of many martial arts classes, students are encouraged to engage in some form of meditation, whether of the formal variety (e.g. *mokuso*) or a more organic kind. Whatever ritual they perform in order to get themselves into the right frame-of-mind, it is undeniable that the fewer distractions—both internal and external—the greater the ability to manage the task at hand. Don't just see; actively look. Don't just hear; actively listen. Don't just touch; actively feel.

2. **Practice**: Another factor in this equation is familiarity with the actions in play—both your own and those of the opponent. Automatic/autonomic actions are much faster than conscious machinations, and this not only brings the desires result more quickly; it also frees up valuable head-space to devote to the first factor (focus).

3. **Mindset**: Several scientific studies have noted that subjects who are confident, optimistic, and cheerful report feeling that they have more time to complete clinical tests than their more apprehensive, pessimistic, disconsolate counterparts.

4. **Timing**: Between every beat there is a space, and according to Bram, it is in these spaces, and not the beats, where the real magic is to be discovered; where the beat can be stolen. To the uninitiated, a set of techniques may look seamless, but the Modular practitioner knows that there are intervals between action and reaction concealed within the flow, which can be employed and exploited. As Remy Presas once told Bram: *"I discovered the Flow between redonda (circular striking) and sinawali (a series of three forward strikes)."*

> **PRECEPT: SLOW IS SMOOTH; SMOOTH IS FAST.**

Kinetic Energy: You must develop a feel for the tool and a feel for the art. With the tool, you don't deploy a kinetic opener by slamming or yanking it. The correct feeling is more akin to walking through a turnstile or releasing a seatbelt—move fluidly and with confidence and purpose. Same thing with the art.

Order in Chaos: A wise Master used to despise the expression: "I have no idea." He would invariably reply: *"If you think about it, you always have at least **some** idea."*

The Art of The Blade

PROBABILITIES

You are ***either*** right or left-handed (or ambidextrous) ***all of the time***	[Y= R/L/L&R]	100%
Probability that at least ***one of any two*** combatants will be right-handed	[R↔R/R↔L]	99%
Probability that ***your opponent*** will be right-handed	[Y↔R]	90%
Probability that ***any two*** combatants will ***both*** be right-handed	[R↔R]	80%
Probability that at least ***one of any two*** combatants will be left-handed	[L↔R/L↔L]	20%
Probability that ***your opponent*** will be left-handed	[Y↔L]	10%
Probability that ***any two*** combatants will ***both*** be left-handed	[L↔L]	1%
Probability that ***one of any two*** combatants will be ambidextrous	[?↔R&L/R&L↔?]	2%
Probability that ***your opponent*** will be ambidextrous	[Y↔L&R]	1%
Probability that ***any two*** combatants will ***both*** be ambidextrous	[L&R, L&R]	0.1%

"How far is it from the earth to the moon?" Perhaps you happen to know the precise answer to this question, but even if you don't, at a minimum, you know it's not as far as the next galaxy over, nor as close as the corner store, and those bookends at least provide an analytical starting point...

As notorious heavyweight champion Mike Tyson is reputed to have said, *"Everyone has a plan until they get punched in the mouth."* Chaos is embedded in the texture of combat. And everything a fighter can do to diminish that chaos improves his chances of victory. This is the foundation of such principles as Bram's two grips, three angles, four perspectives, and the permutations and combinations thereof. Even if you are targeted by an unpredictable knife-wielding attacker, you still know a few things:

1. Statistically speaking, it is likely to be a right-hander;
2. Statistically speaking, it is likely to be a man;
3. He can only be holding the blade in forward or reverse grip;
4. If he is intent on killing you, he is likely to stab for the torso;
5. If his intent is to terrorize, injure, or test, he is likely to slash;
6. Slashes can be vertical, diagonal, or horizontal;
7. The most common slash is descending diagonal right-to-left.

Thus, from a universe of *possibilities*, you have now already narrowed the attack down to approximately six *probabilities* (all of which employ trajectories which fall roughly within your upper-left quadrant). And *that's* a pretty good start, because you now have at least *some idea* of how to prepare to defend.

THE QUADRANTS

The defensive zones which a combatant must protect can be broadly categorized as upper-left, upper-right, lower-left, and lower-right. For ease of employment, these zones are identified from the *attacker's* point-of-view, so that there is no need to translate to compensate for mirror imaging.

- **ULZ [upper-left zone]:** Right side of the opponent's head/thorax;
- **URZ [upper-right zone]:** Left side of the opponent's head/thorax;
- **LLZ [lower-left zone]:** Right side of the opponent's stomach/legs;
- **LRZ [lower-right zone]:** Left side of the opponent's stomach/legs.

✝ **Thrust to Torso:** The best block is *always* not to be there, and this is especially true when defending against an edged tool. Thus, the Modular System teaches the student to avoid a direct thrust by body-shifting to a forty-five-degree angle. Not to be confused with the act of avoiding the attack, it is also important to control the thrust using a drop-tip right-to-left parry with the blade. Like a closed umbrella block against an overhead strike, this drop-tip technique (sometimes called "a pendulum block") wards off a center-line attack and allows the practitioner to "reach through the hole" with the live hand to contact and counter-cut the opponent.

✝ **Diagonal Slash in ULZ:** It's never a good idea to try to intercept steel with flesh. Accordingly, in addition to body-shifting out of range, the Modular practitioner intercepts the opponent's striking hand (wrist) with the edge of the tool and then makes contact with the live hand before counter-cutting…

3,300,000 YEARS AFTER THE LAKE TURKANA CORE-FLAKES WERE USED BY PROTO-HUMANS AS MATTER SEPARATORS, STONE (OBSIDIAN) STILL MAKES FOR THE SHARPEST EDGE…

FINAL THOUGHTS

† **1-4-12** is really **Sinawali**. It's the triangular core of Single Sinawali and Sil Lum Tao. It's the same as Wing Chun Wu Sao, Pak Sao, Fook Sao, Huen Sao (repeat). It contains the core biomechanical movements and teaches how to intercept, to counter, and to control space and range.

† **"Backwards"** is just using your *left* hand to do *right* hand motions; **"Backward-Backwards"** is using your *right* hand to do *left* hand motions. Keep in mind: Remy Presas and I are/were both left-handed!

† **Figure 8** explains use of the edge in reverse grip—it shows *why* the blade intercepting the attack in reverse grip is in the same position as in forward grip.

† Knife *makers* think in terms of *blade* geometry; knife *fighters* think in terms of **body** geometry. By stepping off line to the right and pivoting left 45°, you can both take your opponent's target out of range (say, your left shoulder) and at the same time put *your* target (say, his left shoulder) within range of your knife hand (right hand).

† *All* **guns** are loaded; *all* knives are sharp—don't put anything you don't want cut in front of the blade. Unless you have a big red "S" on the front of your costume, remember the First Commandment: Steel cuts flesh!

† Don't become **hypnotized by the blade**. If the blade/blade-hand is trapped, you need to do something with the other hand.

† These are some of the foundational principles of the system that I have designed for you. As you make your journey through the terrain of Modular, I encourage you to **"make it your own,"** (as Remy used to say). That way, we *both* win. And here is some sustenance for you along the way...

† When you reach what you think is the border in this system (or the edge of the world in real life), keep going—**borders are just jumping-off points.**

† **The blade will show you the truth.**

† All students of this art are part of my family...

A Note From Bram To Future Generations

This book is about me and my methodology for designing and using knives. My unique perspective also applies to how I see my legacy:

When my time comes, my wife, Nova Bella Modequillo Frank, will become the legal owner of all my intellectual property (patents, copyrights, registries, trademarks, assignments, etc...) as well as the parent company: Dragon Nails and CSSD/SC. However, Nova does not practice martial arts.

Accordingly, in order to keep my martial legacy alive (Tactical/Combat Anis, the main training methodology of Modular, and use of the blade and bolo) the main licensees for use of my logos, terminology, and methodology will be the following: Mish Handwerker as the inheritor of these arts, with Amy Kirschner as the guiding soul, and Peter Hobart as the chronicler of the art.

As some of you may know, I don't think like others, so in keeping with my modular color scheme, I visualize Mish as the red (1-4-12, the hub), Amy as the blue (2-3-12, the counter/soul), and Peter as the yellow (1-2-2, the connecting thread).

I have also decided to establish a board to assist this core Triad:

Among the Board members, I see David Giddings—my longtime Modular teaching companion and private student—as the purple (5-2-4, bolo); Jason May—with his years of sword and firearms experience and his long history as a private student in Modular and bolo—as the black (adding perspective, which makes the picture "pop"); and John and Michelle Ralston—given to me by Remy, very experienced, and both loving and loved—as the white (subtle tinting and focus).

• Tom Gallo and Ed Frawley are special to me—we have common interests and are close both physically and spiritually—and because of our shared love of Dr. Suess, I see this pair as "CRMIPT #1" and "CRMIPT #2."

• Edessa and Rob Ramos—with their amazing real-world experience—are the soul of my combatives. They know what it is to use Modular, as Remy used to say, "in real."

• And speaking of the chaos of combat, I see my nephew, Chris Chiu—who inherited his father Bruce's legendary Arnis skills—as the embodiment of this elemental force. Chaos cannot be given form or defined by action.

- Finally, Thomas Lehmann is my senior student and my adopted brother. Over decades of teaching together, he came to know me, my system, and my methodology as it evolved (from being beaten up all over the world)! I visualize him as the Red Unicorn.

Thank you all for your love and support in creating this book. And remember: I am manifested into my methodology and into the steel of my knives. In this way, I will always be with you…

Grandmaster Bram Frank

♦ **STEPHEN K. DOWD** ♦
—EDITOR, FMA DIGEST—

I have known Bram Frank since 2005, when I met him at a martial arts event in Anaheim, California. Since then, I have talked with him many times, both electronically and in person. Bram often teaches large numbers of students at seminars. He is one who thrives in crowds. They feed off his energy. Not unlike a rock star; the bigger the crowd the more the juices flow! For him, it's no different from teaching several combative units at a time. As he always tells his students, this is not rocket science. This is a "train the trainer" methodology that allows beginners to learn alongside advanced students. It's easy to learn and everyone can 'get it' very quickly.

Bram's CSSD/SC approaches teaching self-defense skills with a clear mandate: If it's not reality-based, don't do it. *"I believe in tool-based self-defense,"* Bram declares. Everyone has the God-given right to defend themselves against attack. And such skills should work effectively for the little girl, the old guy, and the young lady, not just the muscular jock. Therefore, it's got to be simple, direct and essential. Self-defense has to be based on Common Sense even if that element is really not so common.

His accomplishments as Grandmaster of CSSD/SC Conceptual Arnis/Tactical Arnis, Director/ Founder of CSSC/SC Tactical Modular Systems, Chief Edged Weapons Instructor for S2-CIS-KKp Security, Common Sense Self-defense / Street Combat instructor are remarkable and showcase his expertise in Filipino Martial Arts as a promotor, teacher, and representative.

Bram is known throughout the world so it is only right to say a few things about the man himself (for which I thank Senior Guro Edessa Ramos, a long-time friend, "sister," and student of Bram Frank). He is a first generation personal student of Professor Remy A. Presas. The first time he saw Professor Presas, he said to himself, this was a martial arts genius; a true "master" of what he did. The day he met his teacher, he knew immediately that this was what he wanted to learn and the man he wanted to learn from. He had found his muse, his master, his mentor. Professor Presas was the one who told Bram to learn slowly by working hard until the art was really his, to be patient, to understand how important it is to be smooth in order to be fast, and soft in order to be strong. This master showed him that by training slowly, one can see, understand, and master the 'whys' of the concepts. Modern Arnis and Professor Presas showed Bram how to think conceptually: *"You are already there. It is all the same! You must understand and feel the flow."* And Bram said to himself, *"Gee, that's how I thought martial arts and fighting should be."* Thus began his odyssey.

Bram attributes his conceptual method of teaching to Professor Presas: *"Bram... do you see the differences? Yes? Good... Can you now see it's all the same? It's the same difference!"* Professor Presas's way of teaching demanded that you think, that you actually use your mind, that you see the connections. He used to say that the key was translation; that Modern Arnis allowed one to translate between the tool and the empty hand. To him, it was important to understand the art at a functional level. He encouraged Bram to teach from day one, telling him: *"Go teach what I taught you, for in teaching you will learn fastest, and find out what you really know, and know what you really need to learn."*

Combat must be simple. During a confrontation, memory gives way to instinct, which quickly devolves into the animal response of survival. Knife fighting is a totally different matter. Bram's approach is the modular combative reaction and skills system with an edged tool. It involves self-defense response (SDR) with a blade or edged tool. The Modular system provides a reasonable, ethical, and moral response to a personal attack using an edged tool. *"I don't teach people to 'fight with knives'. I do teach people how to save their lives and the lives of their loved ones while using an edged tool."*

Some approaches to knife teaching should be viewed with concern. These often involve non-users telling potential users what to do. It's dangerous to spread urban martial arts myths about knife usage. People tend to forget: Knives cut flesh. Always. Teaching must involve the responsible, ethical, and moral use of blade, and an understanding of what edged tools really do. People who have no knife experience should not dictate or teach knife usage. Those who have never really cut anything, never hunted, never worked in a kitchen, should not ask people to wade in and get cut. *"Would you learn driving from someone who had never driven a car? Would you let a person who never used a firearm teach you firearm safety?"*

I have been told by many that it is exciting to be a student of Bram Frank. It's exciting to realize after some time how one has evolved. The realization always comes as a surprise, for the process is smooth and the development is subtle. Once the teacher has shown the student the doorway, and the student has discovered the key that opens it, a whole new world opens up. It is obvious from his training methodology that Bram aims to create instructors—*"Instructors who are better than I am,"* he humbly adds. He wants his students to think, to understand, and to know that all things change while simultaneously remaining the same. Bram is like a parent who wants his children to do better than him, to surpass him. He follows the footsteps of his teacher, Remy Presas, who wanted his students to make the art part of their own styles.

◆YOUR JOURNAL◆
The Most Important Book

In your training, the most important book is the one you write yourself. Accordingly, the following few pages, intended to be employed in conjunction with training from a certified instructor, list the modules in the MBC² system in order and provide space for you to add your own notes regarding each core concept:

_____

_____

_____

_____

_____

_____

_____

_____

_____

MODULE I: PERSPECTIVES [HISTORY AND TERMINOLOGY]

MODULE II: 1-4-12 DRILL [STANDARD, BACKWARD, REVERSE]

Module III: Cutting [Intent, Displacement, Bio-mechanics]

MODULE IV: BODY SHIFTING [SPACING AND STRUCTURE]

Module V: Bone-on Bone Blocking

Module VI: 1-2-2 Drill [TRANSITIONS]

Module VII: Decision and Switch Points

MODULE VIII: 2-3-12 DRILL

Module IX: 5-2-4 Drill

MODULE X: DISARMING

Appendix A—Selected Designs

During his career, Bram Frank has turned out many blade designs, often working in conjunction with some of the most well-known knife companies in the world. As a devoted student of the late Remy Presas and the Filipino Martial Arts, Bram often employs nomenclature drawn from the patterns practiced in this beautiful, flowing method of self-defense.

The following examples are members of the '*Gunting* Family':

THE ESCALATOR (ORIGINALLY *'THE GUNTING'*)

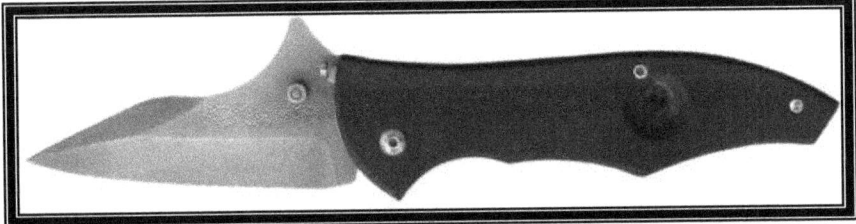

The original design from the mid-1990s, initially intended simply to be called "the *Gunting*," it eventually became known as "the Escalator" and was the first member of this family. This model had a ramp, but with no opening of any kind.

THE *LAPU LAPU*

The *Lapu Lapu* (named for a famous Filipino Datu) is clearly a member of the *Gunting* family but its handle is more like a pistol grip and it is the first *Gunting* to possess proud liners and the puzzle lock.

THE *TUSOK*

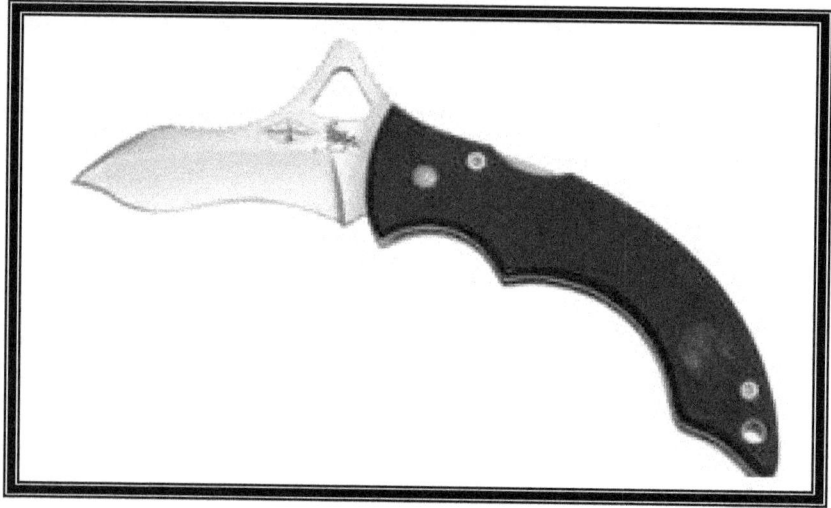

The *Tusok*—meaning "little poke"—is the little sister of the family, and was designed both with and for women.

THE *DESANGUT*

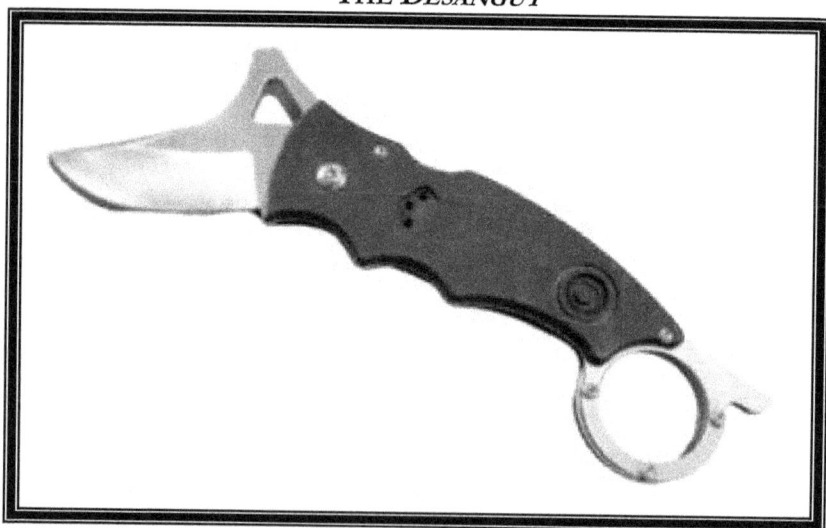

If you want to see Bram go from zero-to-sixty in two seconds flat, try telling him that the *karambit* is the true native fighting knife of the Philippines! He will quickly set you straight, explaining that it is actually the *sangut*, which can cut forward and reverse with its easy grip change mechanism. Bram's version of this formidable weapon pays tribute to *sangut* master Edessa Ramos by adding the *"de"* before *"sangut,"* and features a "finger bramp" for better grip control and striking/trapping applications.

THE SPYDERCO *GUNTING* [BLACK]

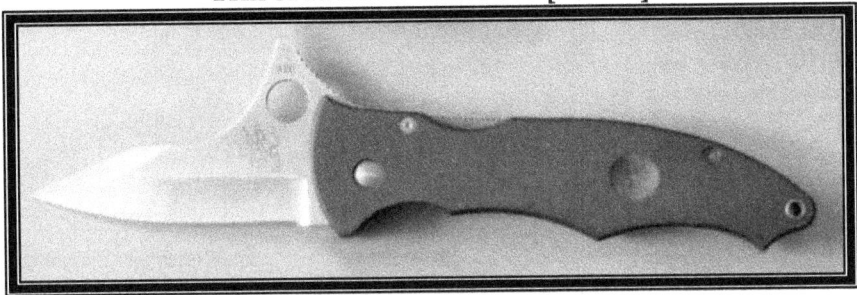

The product of an early collaboration with established knife manufacturer Spyderco, this live blade features many of the mechanisms for which Bram is so well known, including: Kinetic opening (the "Bramp"); tactile indexing; and the spoon clip.

THE SPYDERCO TRAINER DRONE [RED]

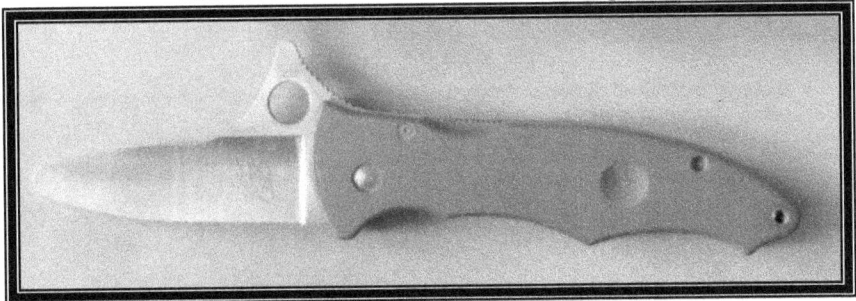

Like most of Bram's tools, the Spyderco *Gunting* has a red training version with almost identical dimensions but an unsharpened blade.

THE SPYDERCO WORKING TOOL [BLUE]

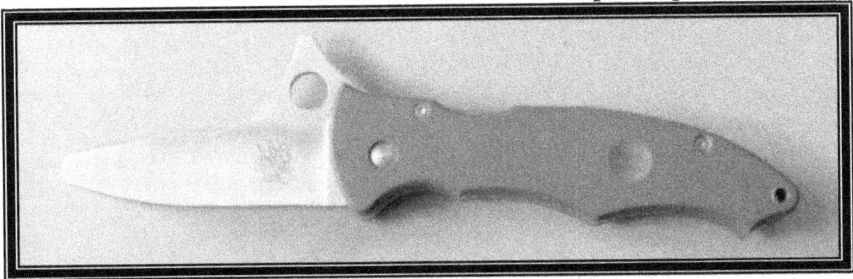

This same basic design was also offered by Spyderco in a blue "working tool" version, similar to the latter-day CRMIPT.

THE *ABANIKO* [FIXED]

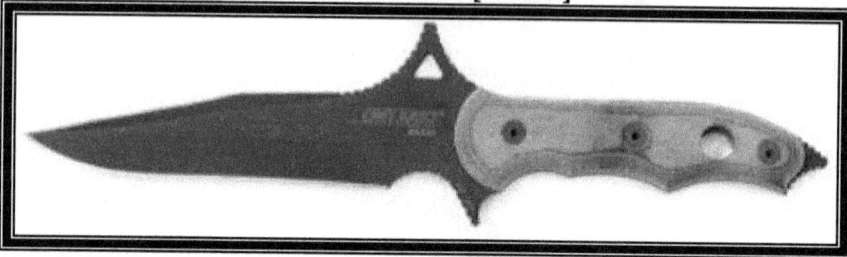

No longer in production, the *Abaniko*—especially the seven-inch version—is one of the most sought-after blades in the knife world. A favorite among military special operators, on those rare occasions when someone is willing to part with one, it will sell for many times its original price, or, on occasion, be passed along as a treasured gift. Should you ever come across one in your travels (and not want it for yourself), please let Bram or the publisher know right away!

THE *REDONDA* [FIXED]

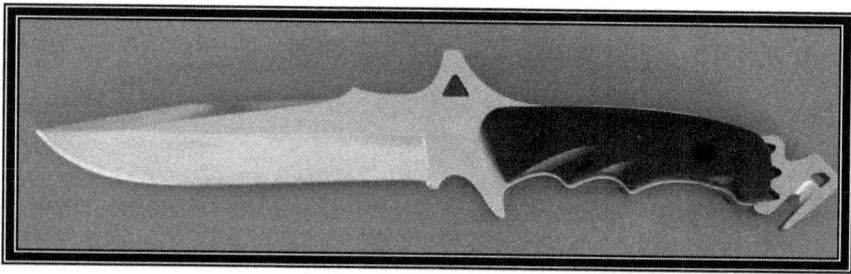

Still on the horizon, Bram's big blade will likely be back by popular demand in the not-too-distant future. What he has in mind is the *Redonda*—a monster of a fixed blade that still captures the elegance of the art.

Appendix B—Selected Endorsements

UNITED STATES CENTRAL COMMAND
7115 SOUTH BOUNDARY BOULEVARD
MACDILL AIR FORCE BASE, FLORIDA 33621-5101

15 November, 2004

Director of Joint Security

Mr. Bram Frank
Director/Founder
Common Sense Self Defense/Street Combat
3665 East Bay Drive Suite 204
Largo, FL 33771

Dear Mr. Frank:

On behalf of the United States Central Command Joint Security Element, I would like to thank you for volunteering your time to instruct our Protective Services Agents on the use of the Gunting-Crimpt Modular Tactical Knife. I received much positive feedback from the students regarding the effectiveness of the system and the quality of instruction. I am confident that the training that you provided will make an immediate and significant impact in the hand-to-hand proficiency of our personnel.

I greatly appreciate your on-going commitment to providing outstanding training to our service members. I hope that, in the future, you will continue to offer your depth of personal knowledge and experience for the further development of our agents in this very effective personal defense system.

Respectfully,

ALBERT F. RIGGLE
Colonel, USAF
Director of Joint Security

The Art of The Blade

DEPARTMENT OF THE TREASURY
BUREAU OF ALCOHOL, TOBACCO AND FIREARMS

241 37th Street
3rd Floor
Brooklyn, New York 11232

Bram Frank
Director CSSD/SC
3665 East Bay Drive
Suite 204-#233
Largo, FL 33771-1965

Bram:

As usual your training program is right on. It is exactly what we at the ATF need to know to survive with edged weapons or as you say edged tools. All of us who attended at the training programs, the ATF, Secret Service, Coast Guard, NYPD and DEA came away with real useful knowledge. Your Modular training program for use with edged tools and impact tools is the *tops*. I really like the Abaniko fixed blades but the GUNTING System is the best thing I've seen for LE. With all LE and Agents carrying knives, your Gunting – CRMIPT should be the required carry. I agree with the magazines that it might be the best LE tool ever designed.
I am talking with Special Agent Angel Cassanova, our CQC instructor who trained with you about implementing this as SOP with the ATF Special Agents to use your Modular system.
I also want to tell you the two Modular Instructor Courses I attended with you are brilliant. You teach exactly what we need to know and I'm amazed at how quickly I got the grasp of your new *Learn in 6 teach in 12* program. I look forward to sharing this with more Federal agencies and I'm putting in the orders for purchasing your knives, trainers and DVD training programs. Again your idea that each agent has a trainer and DVD program to go with their live blades is right on the money. Your vision in watching out for our learning and liability is equal to your excellence in your physical training!

Thank you!

Arnold Allen
Special Agent

WWW.ATF.TREAS.GOV

U.S. Department of Justice
Immigration and Naturalization Service

BPA/20/3.4

Office of the Chief Patrol Agent

U.S. Border Patrol Academy
Glynco, Georgia 31524

October 5, 2001

Mr. Bram Frank, Director
Common Sense Self Defense/Street Combat
233
3665 East Bay Drive
Suite 204
Largo, Florida 33771-1765

Dear Mr. Frank:

    As usual, it was a pleasure participating in another one of your instructor seminars on Combat and Modern Arnis tactics for law enforcement officers. The past 30 hours of seminar instruction have proven to be the most practical close-quarters-combat training that our unit has received.

    We were slightly apprehensive when we first contacted you regarding a specialized training program, especially in regards to edged weapons. Our first attempt to secure some training insight concerning the knife culture had been disappointing, as the majority of the experts' responses were well outside of acceptable law enforcement use-of-force parameters.

    Additionally, although law enforcement agencies have traditionally taught knife defense, we wanted to consider the offensive tactics that potential knife-wielding assailants would likely utilize against our officers. We felt that familiarity with the offensive tactics would assist us in identifying adequate defense and counter-moves in edged weapon situations.

    Your program of common sense defensive and counter-offensive tactics blends perfectly with our existing use-of-force model. The Arnis tactics build upon our established law enforcement training approach to pressure point control, empty-hand restraint techniques, and collapsible steel baton deployment.

    Comments from all of the law enforcement participants were favorable, citing both the practical applications and the fit with established techniques. The high level of officer enthusiasm will mean that we will be requesting additional instructor-level seminars. As the word spreads, we can also expect that the class size will expand to accommodate interest from both state and local law enforcement officers.

The Art of The Blade

UNITED STATES SPECIAL OPERATIONS COMMAND
PROTECTIVE SERVICES DETAIL
7701 TAMPA POINT BOULEVARD
MACDILL AIR FORCE BASE, FLORIDA 33621-5323

SMO-PSD

2 January 2004

MEMORANDUM FOR: CRITICAL INTERVENTION SERVICES AND S-2 SAFETY AND INTELLIGENCE INSTITUTE, 1261 SOUTH MISSOURI AVENUE, CLEARWATER, FLORIDA 33756.

SUBJECT: Advanced Training

1. Thank you for the opportunity to train with the S-2 Institute. The Gunting Close Range Medium Impact Tool / Edged Weapons Seminar hosted by S-2, and instructed by Bram Frank and his agency, Common Sense Self Defense-Street Combat, was extremely useful in our mission and enjoyed by my entire staff. S-2 and Bram Frank have broadened our combative and defensive skills and added an entirely new level of less than lethal force to our arsenal. I am confident that the skills gained from this seminar will significantly add to our readiness and ensure mission success. The Training methodology taught to us by Mr. Frank will allow us to teach others, successfully and quickly. His new design for fixed tactical blades the Abaniko, facilitates the training process and we look forward to using both the trainers and live blades in the future for our operations along with his Gunting-CRMIPT. His training program of a Train the Trainer methodology is unique in that it's a concept driven teaching unit. It complies with **one mind, many tools** philosophy of the Military. All of the functional moves are based on gross motor skills and it allows us to change from Impact Tool to edged tool to firearm without changing our training. It might be the best Extreme CQC I have ever trained in!

2. In addition to the above-mentioned seminar, I personally give thanks to S-2 and Critical Intervention Services for the opportunity to attend the Anti-terrorism Officer (ATO) training sessions. In all of my travels and training, military and civilian, I rarely have had the pleasure of encountering such professional instructors and presentations. The knowledge possessed and demonstrated by the instructor staff sets the bar for all civilian training agencies to follow. The training you are providing to the security personnel at Critical Intervention Services (CIS), military personnel and law enforcement professionals, is unmatched by civilian readiness training for the war on terror.

3. It has truly been a privilege and a pleasure to train with such professionals and it is my sincere hope and intention to build a partnership with S-2 and CSSD/SC as a training resource in the future for my teams of LE officers and Military Ops. I have already brought Bram Frank over to the Base to train my teams onsite and will continue to do so. I have also brought him over the fence to CENTCOM notice.

4. Bram Frank and his knife designs need to be mentioned specifically starting with his Gunting Tool system.. The tool is the first one of its kind that I or my team, have ever seen. A tool that allows us to go from Non lethal, to less than lethal, and if needed move to lethal force mode. It is a tool designed for the Law Enforcement community for it seems to follow our standard model of the Force Continuum. I want to thank Bram Frank for understanding and designing this tool to meet our needs. It just might be the best less than lethal tool ever designed for LE-Military applications. The Kinetic Opening feature is unique and amazingly fast. It might be the fastest surest opening device I've ever seen on a tactical folder. There is no other opening device like it on the market; for whether using impact or Ramp opening with gloves on, the Gunting opens immediately. This feature alone will save lives. The other features are amazing as well. The spoon clip on the tool, as Mr. Frank calls it, is matched up with an indented, indexing point in the handle, which certainly makes changing grips from forward to reverse extremely sure and easy. In reverse grip the Ramp acts as a hand stopper to prevent one's hands from sliding onto the blade... I have seen Mr. Frank enact handcuffing and control procedures by trapping the wrists and fingers with the Ramp of the Gunting. The design of the handle is so ergonomic, that my team and myself can write notes, use a cell phone or access other tools, like handcuffs, while the Gunting is in use in our hand already.
For up close and personal usage, such as in EP-Security work, this tool is fantastic. It allows for discreet impact, control, trapping & restraint if needed.

Due to the CRMIPT's limited non lethal action, the Gunting's ability to go from non lethal to lethal and back again, and both with a simple training program, I see a way to close the loop on SOP training and liability of usage. I read that Officer Massad Ayoob, tone of our countries leading *Use of force* Experts has called the system & design a historic event in the world of LE tools. SWAT Magazine Police review called it *the best less than lethal tool ever designed for LE.* I think I agree.
I see the Gunting tool saving many lives and protecting others in the future!

As for Bram Franks new fixed blade? As a Military person I can tell you it is the finest Tactical Knife I have ever encountered. It is made by Onraio knives a manufacturer with long ties to our Military. It is designed to function under gross motor skill situations; a very common occurrence for Military and Law Enforcement. The handle directs one to the cutting edge, it is designed to not come loose in the operator's hand and it is simplistic in it's use. The Abaniko is basically a Gunting on steroids and it can do all the same trapping and restraint moves of a Gunting *without using lethal force.*

Bram has backed that up with a new Modular training program. It is a program which contains not only hands on training, but training Drones, written program, and a video training program (DVD) back up. The Modular training program allows my team to be in reverse grip, forward grip, left handed or right handed, and it all becomes the same.

My team and I are very impressed!

Thank you again.

JERRY D. WHITE
Agent, Protective Services Detail
Advanced Training Section

The Art of The Blade

PSC 812 Box 3220 Slot 190
FPO AE 09627-3220
Cell: 011-39-339-775-1392
COMM: 011-39-09586-2782
DSN: 314-624-2782
e-mail: pmtg01@yahoo.com
kashinot@nassig.sicily.navy.mil

20 December 2004

Mr. Bram Frank
CSSD/SC Training Systems
2274 State Road, Suite 580
Clearwater, Florida 33763

Dear Mr. Frank;

    Thank you for taking the time to come to Naval Air Station Sigonella to hold a seminar this past May. As a thirteen-year Military Police professional for both the Army and Navy, and a twenty-year student of the martial arts, I found your techniques and training methods to be extraordinary. Your Modular Blade Concepts (MBC) curriculum is by far the most practical training methodology for edged weapons that I have had the pleasure to experience.
    The Gunting and CRMIT tools and the innovative training system that you have built around them brings new validity to pain compliance techniques and opens up a new dimension in defensive tactics for police and security professionals. I am highly impressed with the versatility and immediate effectiveness of the Gunting tool. My Gunting has taken a place on my duty belt and has become an indispensable multi-purpose tool and force multiplier.
    It is can see that both methods are very compatible with military train-the-trainer type programs. The focus on gross motor movement in both training systems allows for the material to be learned quickly and retained with a modest amount of follow-on training. I have personally applied MBC and Gunting training methodologies in my martial arts classes as well as in my unit's defensive tactics training, and I have seen how CSSD training concepts speed up the learning process. I have also applied these methods on the job. The bottom line is that this stuff works.
    I whole-heartedly recommend your training and products to anyone interested in finding simple and effective empty hand and edged/impact weapon combatives. By all means, feel free to share this letter and my contact information with anyone seeking further information from you about CSSD/SC. Keep up the good work. We're looking forward to seeing you back in Sicily next year.

                    Sincerely,

                    Timothy P. Kashino
                    MA1(SW), USN
                    Patrol Section Supervisor

West Central Executive Protection Services

August 14, 2005

Bram Frank
Director - Common Sense Self Defense
3665 East Bay Drive
Suite 204 #233
Largo, FL 33771-1965

Dear Mr. Frank,

As President of West Central Executive Protection Services and a 26-year LEO veteran, I would like to commend you on both your training system and the Gunting – CRMIPT tools. A major concern of mine has always been the ability to control a situation without having to resort to lethal force. I believe that your system has solved that problem. I am especially impressed with the simplicity and ease in which I can train my staff and others using your Modular CQC system. Yours is one of the only systems that address the issue of motor skill deterioration during stress. The natural body motions involved work well in real life critical situations. I have experienced and witnessed first hand the total effectiveness of the Gunting and CRMIPT tools. I give my highest recommendation to your training system, and the Gunting - CRMIPT.

In my opinion, you are truly a pioneer in the field of close quarter defense. I am looking forward to working closely with the CSSD/SC organization in the future.

Sincerely,

Thomas H. Walters
President
West Central Executive Protection Services.

The Art of The Blade

Grandmaster Bram Frank CSSD/SC
Master of the Blade
Master of Arms—Filipino Blade
Master of Israeli Filipino Knife Combatives

In Honor of **Grandmaster Bram Frank**: his decade of teaching the Art of the Blade, Tactical Knife, and Arnis in Israel, his dedication to the State of Israel, its preservation, soldiers, agents and citizens, His continuing and ongoing Tactical Knife program of Knife-Counter Knife camp in Israel known as the **Commandments of Steel**, **Grandmaster Bram Frank** is hereby acknowledged and recognized as the **Father of Israeli Knife and Knife Combatives**.

To Grandmaster Bram:
Let your life's work of the BLADE, at long last be recognized around the world as it is here in Israel; and may you find true happiness. I feel that you are a TRUE Samurai and can only wish you Health, Happiness and most of all Peace with yourself and the World. Your family in Israel calls you **the Lion of Judah**. You are my brother in the Martial arts and you are worthy of the title: **Father of Israel Knife Combatives**.

Your Friend & colleague:

Dennis
May 2007

Dennis Hanover: Survival JuJitsu

DR. DENNIS HANOVER
10TH DAN VICE PRESIDENT
OF THE ORIGINAL E.J.J.U
INDUCTED GRANDMASTER
AND FOUNDER OF
DENNIS SURVIVAL JU-JITSU
BY THE WORLD HEAD
FAMILY SOKESHIP COUNCIL
INTERNATIONAL HALL OF FAME

Dr. Dennis Hanover
Father of Israel Martial Art: Dennis Survival JuJitsu

Dr. Dennis Hanover, 10th Dan, Soke
Grand Master
Life President of
Dennis Survival Ju Jitsu
&
The Original E.J.J.U

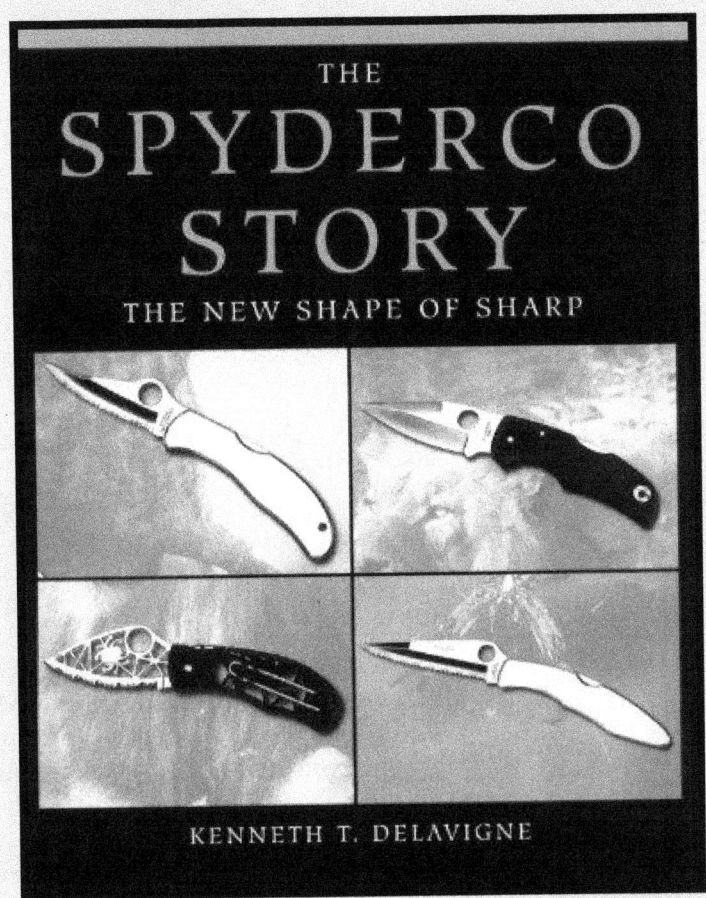

EXCERPT FROM LETTER FROM KENNETH DELAVIGNE TO BRAM

"...MBC would seem to represent the same kind of paradigm shift for the tool industry as the hold, clip, serrations, and even the original blade locks were.... [O]nce one of these shifts has taken place, there is no going back; the future is forever different. MBC, meaning the tools, the philosophy, the mental attitude, and the training, will probably save many lives and avoid a lot of legal fees wasted defending against phony deadly-weapon charges. And Spyderco's name will be linked with it.

When I think of some of the collaborators--great craftsmen with narrow fields of view--and compare them with Bram, the comprehensiveness of his field of view stands out: the focus shifts from beautiful knives to a world-view encompassing many different tools and a philosophy of their use. I see this as Spyderco's fourth phase. Mazel tov! Ken"

The Art of The Blade

GLOSSARY
["Bram-speak"]

† **1-4-12:** First give-and-take drill [pattern: high right/low left/overhead]

† **1-2-2:** Second give-and-take drill [pattern: high right/high left/high left]

† **2-3-12:** Third give-and-take drill [pattern: high left/low left/overhead]

† **5-2-4:** Fourth give-and-take drill [pattern: thrust/high left/low left]

† **Bio-Mechanical Cutting:** Shutting down the opponent damaging pulleys (bones), cables (tendons) and nerves (control switches) ["Black Knight Syndrome"]

† **Body shifting:** Body rotation using stance; moving off center line; pivoting on the balls of the feet.

† **Chaos:** Characteristic of true **combat**: Disorganized, chaotic, random, without reason. Modular methodology allows training in simulated chaotic situations and provides structure with which to bring some order to chaos.

† **Checking:** The touch ("Braille") method of controlling the motion of the opponent's limbs.

† **Connecting Thread:** A module that allow shifting from one module to another [1-2-2].

† **CRMIPT:** Close Range Medium ImPact Tool.

† **Decision Point:** Intentional switch to another drill/move.

† **EDC:** <u>E</u>very <u>D</u>ay <u>C</u>arry.

† **Equal Forward:** Both participants in forward grip (tip up).
  [**Unequal Forward:** Attacker in reverse grip/defender forward].

† **Equal Reverse:**	Both participants in reverse grip (tip down).
[**Unequal Reverse:**	Attacker in forward grip/defender reverse].
† **Extensors:**	Tendons and muscles used to extend the fingers or limbs, secondary targets [outside of forearm, front of leg].
† **Flexors:**	Tendons and muscles used to contract the fingers or limbs, primary targets [inside of forearm, back of leg, Achilles tendon].
† **Flow:**	The ability to exist between action and reaction; to find connecting bridges between motions.
† **Grips:**	• **Equal Forward:** Both in forward grip; • **Unequal:** One forward/other in reverse; • **Unequal:** One in reverse/other in forward; • **Equal Reverse:** Both in reverse.
† *Gunting:*	Scissoring action/limb destruction seen in Modern Arnis; escalation in force.
† **High Line:**	Techniques performed (mainly) above arms.
† **Horizontal-Vertical:**	Base move intercept/remove enemy's guard.
† **ICC:**	Intercept Check /Control, Counter.
† **Indexing:**	Points or indents on the handle of a tool.
† **Kinetic Opening:**	Using energy in motion to open a folding tool [like a turnstile].
† **Low Line:**	Techniques performed (mainly) below arms.
† **Measured Force:**	Using the minimum force needed to get the job done [Force Continuum].
† **Modular:**	Using modules of motion (often grouped in easily-absorbable sets of three) for ease of learning.

The Art of The Blade

† **MBC²** Modular Blade Concepts/Martial Blade Craft: An edged tool system of self-defense developed by Bram Frank.

† **Patchwork Quilt:** Description of how modules can be assembled so that each piece is identical yet can be arranged to express personal preferences.

† **Perspectives:** The alternative dimensions of combat:
  • **Standard:** Right to right;
  • **Backwards:** Left to right;
  • **Mirror:** Left to Left;
  • **Backward-Backwards:** Right to Left.

† **PCAT:** Principle, Concept, Application, Technique.

† **ROC:** Reactive Opponent Control.

† **Rounding Cuts:** A way of manipulating a slice on contact so that it curves around a target (like a wrist).

† **SDA:** Single Direct Attack.

† **SDR:** Self Defense Response.

† **SHO:** Single Handed Opener.

† **Stirring:** Using tool or hand to redirect an attack.

† **Switch Point:** Change drill/move in response to barrier.

† **TRT:** Tactical Response Tool.

†

A FINAL PERSPECTIVE CHECK

As *Saint-Exupéry's* fox said to the Little Prince: *"And now here is my secret, a very simple secret…"*

Use a pencil to draw lines connecting each utility to each house without crossing

The Art of The Blade

♦ ABOUT THE AUTHORS ♦

As with any list of acknowledgements, there is a fair chance that the Editors will inadvertently neglect to mention kind and valuable contributions from one source or another. In an effort to avoid any such omission, it should be recognized that this work is the product of many currents in this martial tributary. It is for this—and several other—reasons that authorship is collectively attributed to *Retzev:* "the flow." Having said that, it is appropriate to provide specific recognition for several individuals, without whose assistance this work could not have been completed.

- † **Dan Anderson:** Bram's colleague and friend, himself a living legend.
- † **Chad Bailey:** Longtime student of both Bram and Professor Presas.
- † **Bruce and Chris Chiu:** Bram's colleagues and amazing martial artists.
- † **Stephen K. Dowd:** Senior practitioner and the Editor of FMA Digest.
- † **Eric Filippenko**: Member of the tribe with the heart of a lion.
- † **Tom Gallo & Ed Frawley:** Die-hard fans of the CRMIPT.
- † **Dave Giddings:** Master technician with a gift for explaining.
- † **Mish Handwerker:** Bram's right-hand man in the CSSD/SC program.
- † **Amy Kirschner:** One of Bram's most senior students (and "daughter").
- † **Thomas Lehmann:** Bram's longest standing student; based in Germany.
- † **Jason May:** Master of both long (Japanese) and short (Filipino) blade.
- † **Vince Oller:** Longtime Bram student and world class martial artist.
- † **John and Michelle Ralston:** Loyal senior practitioners of Bram's art.
- † **Edessa Ramos:** Practitioner whose skill has been tested in the crucible.
- † **Tony Torre:** Long standing student of Bram and master martial artist.
- † **Brian Zawilinski:** Bram's colleague and Master of *Tapi-Tapi* (Arnis).
- † **All other contributing students and teachers** of the Art of the Blade.

The Art of The Blade

www.ingramcontent.com/pod-product-compliance
Lightning Source LLC
Chambersburg PA
CBHW051045160426
43193CB00010B/1072